INTERVENTIONS

Interventions is produced on the land of the Wurundjeri people of the Kulin Nation. We acknowledge the Traditional Owners of country throughout Australia and recognise their continuing connection to land, waters and culture. We pay our respects to their Elders past, present and emerging. Their land was stolen, never ceded. It always was and always will be Aboriginal land.

First published 2024 by Interventions Publishers.

Interventions Inc is a not-for-profit, independent, radical book publisher.
For further information:

    www.interventions.org.au
    info@interventions.org.au
    PO Box 963
    Coffs Harbour NSW 2450

Design and layout of cover and interior by Viktoria Ivanova
Images used in cover design and interior of book by Tia Kasambalis

Author: Colleen Bolger

Title: Nothing is normal: Witness to the Greek crisis 2015
ISBN: 978-0-6452535-5-9: Paperback
ISBN: 978-0-6452535-6-6: ebook

© Colleen Bolger 2024

The moral rights of the author have been asserted.

All rights reserved. Except as permitted under the Australian Copyright Act 1968 (for example, a fair dealing for the purposes of study, research, criticism or review), no part of this book may be reproduced, stored in a retrieval system, communicated or transmitted in any form or by any means without prior written permission.

All inquiries should be made to the publisher.

 A catalogue record for this work is available from the National Library of Australia

NOTHING IS NORMAL
Witness to the Greek crisis 2015

COLLEEN BOLGER

INTERVENTIONS

CONTENTS

Publisher's foreword — 1

Introduction — 5

Dispatches from Greece 2015 — 19

Breaking all the rules : 01 July, Wednesday — 25

'Nothing is normal' : 03 July, Friday — 32

Battle lines: 04 July, Saturday — 37

A historic vote, but challenges ahead: 06 July, Monday — 56

Ruptures: 12 July, Sunday — 93

The left responds: 14 July, Tuesday — 116

New battle lines: 17 July, Friday — 126

Turning resignation into resistance: 27 July, Monday — 152

Polarisation in Syriza: 10 August, Monday — 179

The deal is done, but the fight isn't over: 18 August, Tuesday — 185

The defeat of the left, and the recomposition: 27 September, Sunday — 191

Austerity becomes the new reality
An interview with Panos Petrou in August 2023 — 197

Further reading — 213

Glossary — 215

Biographies — 219

PUBLISHER'S FOREWORD

In January 2015, when Greece had been in crisis for half a decade, the left-wing government of Syriza was elected.

In the northern summer, following the announcement by Greek Prime Minister Alexis Tsipras on 27 June that he would call a referendum on the austerity deal proposed by the EU institutions, Colleen Bolger spent several weeks in Greece. She covered the mass events, writing her daily experiences in a series of dispatches published in the Australian socialist newspaper, *Red Flag*, between early July and late September 2015.

This book is an edited version of the original articles. It includes an introduction written by Colleen in July 2023 and a postscript interview with Panos Petrou, a leading Greek socialist, conducted in August 2023.

The Introduction sets the context for readers who may not remember 2015. Colleen explains who the political actors were, discusses the crisis and the aftermath, explores various debates on the left internationally that the Greek experience generated and comments on the relevance of the events a decade later.

The tone changes dramatically when we turn to the second section, 'Dispatches from Greece'. In her daily reports, Colleen takes us through her experiences on the streets and the evolving circumstances. Over the 10 weeks, the excitement of the early days gives way to an outcome that was disappointing and disheartening in many ways. When Colleen ended her dispatches in late September, the longer-term consequences were not yet clear, but the general direction could be seen – and, as Colleen pointed out, the situation on the ground was going to be incredibly difficult.

The third section of the book, 'Austerity Becomes the New Reality', moves forward nearly a decade to the present. Colleen interviewed Panos Petrou in August 2023, and this allows us to use hindsight to draw up a balance sheet. The interview covers what has happened in Greek society and economy in the nearly 10 years since the mass events, including the outcome for the political situation in general and the left formation Syriza in particular. Despite the defeats, Panos ends with a hopeful look at the future: 'Those both inside Syriza and outside Syriza, we are the forces that still can serve as the starting point for something new and more radical.'

Together, the sections form a work that captures the spirit and the political debates of the time and combines them with a more sober, retrospective analysis.

This book is written for the general reader, not the expert. In order to promote readability, we have not given full details of all abbreviations in the main text; all acronyms and abbreviations, explanations of Greek words and details of organisations and political figures are in the Glossary. Similarly, there are few citations and no footnotes. Two books cited in the main text are listed in the Further Reading suggestions.

Interventions would like to thank Ben Hillier for editing the work, Tia Kasambalis for the wonderful photos and Colleen herself for her work on this edition, including the new introduction and the interview with Panos Petrou.

AUTHOR ACKNOWLEDGMENTS
COLLEEN BOLGER

I am very grateful to the comrades who helped me navigate my time in Athens in 2015 by taking the trouble to explain the context of the events that were unfolding, introduce me to people to interview and alert me to events I could attend. In particular, Kevin Ovenden, Panos Petrou, Thanasis Kourkoulas and Sotiris Matarlis were generous with their time and insights. The Keratsini branch of DEA welcomed me joining them in their work. Yiorgios Kokkinaris took the trouble to translate many meetings for me – without which I would have been lost – and became a dear friend.

My comrades in Socialist Alternative closely followed the rise of Syriza and the political situation in Greece between 2012 and 2015. Our understanding of the lessons from this period was greatly enriched by our comradely relationship with DEA. My analysis was shaped by, and sharpened in, those discussions.

Ben Hillier, as an editor, has made me seem a better writer than I am, but his powers can only go so far. My discussions with him and co-editor, Corey Oakley, during this period were invaluable.

Any insights gleaned were only possible through the collaboration and generosity of these comrades. The weaknesses are my own.

ABOUT THE PHOTOGRAPHY
TIA KASAMBALIS

I travelled to Greece in 2015, staying with friends in the heart of Athens. A few weeks after my arrival, Prime Minister Alexis Tsipras announced a referendum on whether the country should accept harsh bailout conditions on international loans to the Greek Government. Tens of thousands of people filled Athens' narrow streets and its historic public squares, demanding an end to austerity. 'OXI!' they chanted. In my Greek–Australian accent and with a newfound passion for socialist politics, I joined in too, chanting, 'OR-HE!'

The photos depicting these demonstrations were taken in late June and early July in the lead-up to, and on the night of, the referendum. They document the anger and frustration of the Greek people. And, for a brief moment, a sense of optimism. The other photos of Athens and its inhabitants are from trips in 2016 and 2018.

INTRODUCTION

I hadn't expected to be in Greece in 2015. I only made plans on the night that Prime Minister Alexis Tsipras called a referendum. The young, Eurocommunist leader of Syriza (Synaspismós Rizospastikís Aristerás – Proodeftikí Simachía, or the Coalition of the Radical Left) asked the people to determine whether to accept 'the memorandum'. A 'Troika' of creditors – the International Monetary Fund, the European Commission and the European Central Bank – had proposed a new loan repayment agreement. The rest of the international left and I had been following the development of Syriza for several years. It was one of the broad left parties in Europe enjoying some success since the global financial crisis of 2007-09. Our interest intensified when Syriza won the national election in January 2015. Now was the test of its claim to be a government of the left and its stated intention of cancelling the country's crippling debt – being paid for with deep cuts to social spending.

Expecting to lose the election, the ruling conservative party, New Democracy, had negotiated to bring forward the loan repayment schedule to put maximum pressure on the incoming government. Syriza was immediately caught in interminable negotiations with the Troika, which people passively watched through media reporting. That changed when an impasse in the negotiations led Tsipras to make a bold call: let the people decide in a referendum whether to accept the creditors' terms. The political terrain would now return to the streets. I took the next plane to Athens.

This collection of articles dates back to that time. They detail my observations about how the crisis manifested; the meaning of the referendum results; and how events tested the left's orientation to Syriza. I was privileged to dance in the streets with people celebrating their victory when 61 percent voted to reject the memorandum. The speed with which Tsipras 'turned the No into Yes', by signing a worse agreement days later, should be part of every revolutionary's arsenal of examples of the uselessness of left-wing leaders who seek compromise with the class enemy.

THE POLITICAL ACTORS

Greece came late to liberal democracy. After the fall of the military junta in 1974, the modern era of Greek politics mirrored liberal democracies throughout the Western world: regular electoral contests pitted a main bourgeois conservative party, New Democracy, against its social democratic counterpart, the Panhellenic Socialist Movement (Panellínio Sosialistikó Kínima, or Pasok). From the 1981 election of Andreas Papandreou, the first Pasok prime minister, the party gained the loyalty of most working-class voters and tended to be the more successful of the two main parties.

Greece's main fascist party, Golden Dawn, peaked at 7 percent of the vote in 2012 and 2015. That it did not win more success out of the crises in this period is thanks in no small part to the left's wider ascendancy and anti-fascist organising. The other party on the right was the Independent Greeks – National Patriotic Alliance (Anexartitoi Ellines; ANEL), a 2012 nationalist split from New Democracy.

The struggle against the dictatorship had provided cadre for all the political formations on the left. The Communist Party of Greece (Kommounistikó Kómma Elládas; KKE) still enjoys prestige from leading the struggle against the fascist occupation during World War II and against the junta installed by the West in the war's aftermath.

Historically, the KKE has been the main party to the left of Pasok. Between 2000 and 2023, it has polled 5–8 percent of the vote. The Communists have a reputation for being highly sectarian, nationalist and conservative, compared with the rest of the left, and these tendencies were on display during the period of Syriza's first government. The KKE's Stalinist legacy also infects the political currents that split from it.

Syriza formed in 2004 on the back of the shift to the left evident in the anti-capitalist movement of the late 1990s and early 2000s and then the antiwar movement between 2001 and 2003. In its first three national elections, Syriza polled 4–5 percent, showing that there was an audience among a radicalising minority. Later, in 2009, a second electoral front formed from groups outside Syriza: Antarsya (Antikapitalistiki Aristeri Synergasia gia tin Anatropi, or Front of the Greek Anticapitalist Left). It was never electorally successful, peaking at 1.1 percent in the polls in January 2015. Debates on the left about which of these two coalitions to relate to feature in these articles.

Syriza contained different currents. The main one was Synaspismós, a Eurocommunist split from the KKE. Surrounding Tsipras was a right-wing cadre from this tradition, whose politics inclined toward compromise and class collaboration. The most pro-business among them came to dominate the negotiations with the Troika, and they sidelined the more radical voices prepared to default if necessary. Among the latter was Yannis

Varoufakis, a brash economist recruited to Syriza to be the finance minister. There were other varieties of left reformists in the coalition, also splits from the KKE or its progeny; the main one was the Left Current, the primary factional opposition to Tsipras's betrayal.

In the 2012 election, Syriza quadrupled its vote and came within 2 percent of New Democracy, which went on to form government. Having established itself as the main opposition party, and with the economic and social crisis deepening during New Democracy's term of government, Syriza became the government in waiting.

THE CRISIS

The 2007–08 global financial crisis and the so-called Great Recession that followed was the largest coordinated capitalist collapse since the 1930s. The crisis affected hundreds of millions of workers as it spread from the US housing market into credit markets, job markets and global trade. In *Why not default? The political economy of sovereign debt* (e-book p. 155), Jerome Roos summarised the fallout in Greece that began in 2009:

> Coming barely a year after the...start of the global financial crisis, the announcement by the incoming [Pasok] government of George Papandreou that its predecessors had been cooking the books and that the new administration faced a momentous €31 billion shortfall in annual public revenue struck like a bombshell. With the European banking system still reeling and the global economy in the throngs of its steepest downturn since the Great Depression, investors reacted to the news by taking flight.
>
> Although Greece only made up about 2 percent of the total economic output of the European Union,

its government owed about €300 billion to various private lenders at home and abroad, raising fears that a disorderly Greek default might undermine the stability of the wider European banking system, lead to financial contagion across the periphery of the heavily indebted Eurozone, and call into question not just Greece's place within the single currency but the very survival of the monetary union.

Adamant to avoid such a scenario, the EU member states banded together with the European Central Bank and IMF to organize the largest international emergency loans in history to prevent Greece from reneging on its foreign obligations. The onerous conditions attached to the three successive bailout programs sent the Greek economy into a nosedive, with the country entering a deep depression... Losing almost a third of its total economic output and with a quarter of its population out of work, the country experienced one of the most severe contractions of any advanced capitalist economy during peacetime.

The first bailout of €110 billion came in May 2010. The conditions were so onerous that, within a year, Greece needed another bailout. The magnitude of austerity demanded in the two agreements was worth 18 percent of GDP in 2011. The scale of the resulting social and economic crisis led to Papandreou's resignation and the collapse of Pasok. It was clear that Greece would need a third bailout, but Antonis Samaras' New Democracy government – elected in 2012 after the collapse of a national unity government and a short-lived caretaker administration – was reluctant to conclude an agreement before the January 2015 election.

Swept to office on an anti-austerity platform, Syriza immediately plunged into negotiations with the Troika creditors, who used every weapon at their disposal to bring the new government into line. They withheld the last tranche of €7 billion from the second bailout fund and restricted the Greek Government's access to credit. Speculators bet on the insolvency of the Greek banks, leading to a drawing down of deposits and a stock market plunge of more than 40 percent.

The European financial institutions were sending a message: the Greek working class would pay dearly if they rejected the financial system's rules. The Troika's campaign was successful even before Tsipras's final capitulation after the referendum. Within a month of taking office, Tsipras had agreed to an extension of debt repayments, on the promise that his government would take no action contrary to the terms of the previous memorandums. By the end of April, Yannis Varoufakis, the only person in Tsipras's inner circle prepared to default, was sidelined in the negotiations. A document showing that Tsipras was prepared to make huge concessions was leaked to the press in the last days of the June negotiations. The concessions were still rejected by the Troika. Finally, when presented with a 'take it or leave it' deal, Tsipras withdrew from negotiations and called the referendum, advocating that the people vote No to the proposed Troika deal.

CAPITULATION

Yanis Varoufakis writes in his account of the time, *Adults in the Room,* of people stopping him on the street, imploring him to keep the promise not to sign another memorandum. He also tells a story about being summonsed to Tsipras's office on the day Syriza was sworn in and being told that, should they capitulate, they would have to give back the keys to their office. Varoufakis asked Tsipras several times during the negotiations to assure him that that was still the case. He always said yes – until the night of the referendum. It became clear, from the downcast expression on Syriza ministers' faces as they watched the celebrations in Syntagma Square below, that Tsipras had, at best, wanted a thin victory – something he could take as proof that he had to make concessions.

On the day of the referendum, the Greek people gave a resounding *OXI* – a Greek 'No' – to austerity and to more years of suffering. In a betrayal of all those who voted for Syriza in January 2015, and of the millions more who voted *OXI*, Tsipras signed a memorandum within a week of the result. The terms were worse than those offered before the referendum. To consolidate the position, he called a snap election; this successfully purged the party of the remaining left-wing MPs who opposed the capitulation and transformed Syriza into its opposite, from an anti-austerity party to a party embracing and implementing austerity.

WHAT WAS AT STAKE?

Syriza's electoral victory on 25 January 2015 set up a clash with the ruling classes of the European Union and the continent's most powerful financial institutions. It would put to the test the strategy of using capitalist state power to reverse austerity.

A curious thing had happened in the run up to the election. Greece had been the place where class resistance to austerity had been the strongest in Europe. Between 2010 and 2012, there were 10 general strikes against austerity. They were combative, often ending in fierce street confrontations with police around the Hellenic Parliament. However, protests and strikes were less frequent after Syriza almost clinched the election in 2012; they declined further as the 2015 election approached.

Workers had come up against the limits of set-piece 24 or 48-hour general strikes called by their trade unions. The trade union leaders were not prepared to extend the strikes and lead a generalised confrontation to reverse the memorandums. However, Syriza's success suggested another way forward: elect a party that pledged to tear up the rule book. Syriza became a government in waiting, with the hopes of the working class on its shoulders.

At the time, many of us thought it possible that Syriza's election would re-enliven working class self-activity in the streets and workplaces. It had done so when Leon Blum's Popular Front coalition between the French Communist Party and Socialist Party was elected in France in 1936 and when Salvador Allende was elected in Chile in 1973. This did not eventuate. The air of expectation of what Syriza would deliver had substituted for the class struggle for too long for it to revive immediately upon the new government's election.

It was possible to call demonstrations or strikes in defence of Syriza against the Troika or over particular concessions. They might have succeeded, depending on the size of the forces calling them. Instead, the overwhelming focus of people's energy was sucked into their television screens as they watched the next bulletin carrying news of the negotiations. The social contest over the referendum briefly changed that dynamic; but the capitulation came only five days later. There was not nearly enough time to revive the struggle on the streets before demoralisation set in.

The reformist framework of Syriza made some form of capitulation inevitable. Revolutionaries had been preparing for it and were ready when it came. They were instrumental in the split from Syriza by the 53 MPs who opposed the new Memorandum and formed the Popular Unity party.

Nonetheless, the depth of the social crisis and politicisation, combined with the Troika's intransigence, briefly opened the possibility of a further deepening of the crisis – if Greece had defaulted. This would have meant expulsion from the European Union and the reintroduction of a local currency, the drachma, which would have fallen rapidly. This would, as the representatives of the Troika, the press and the Greek capitalists constantly threatened, eviscerate living standards in Greece. However, it would also have raised the prospect of seizing the remaining wealth inside the country through a full-frontal clash with the Greek capitalist class. The crisis would have drawn millions of workers into solving the pressing social questions of keeping hospitals running, distributing food, determining which essential industries needed fuel and materials and resolving countless other questions. A hostile state apparatus would have worked to restore capitalist order, making workers' self-activity necessary.

In this way, walking away from the negotiations with the Troika was setting down a path toward a democratic reorganisation of wealth and society. Syriza's U-turn was predictable, but revolutionaries needed to point toward the alternative of deepening workers' control over the economy.

The Greek Communist Party had the opposite approach. This sizeable and youthful force in Greek politics called on its supporters to abstain in the referendum, on the basis that Tsipras would continue to negotiate and capitulate. That this is exactly how it played out may seem like a vindication of this position. What the following pieces demonstrate is the tragedy of this approach. The KKE ignored the key question that divided society along class lines and stood aside just when the fighting spirit of workers was awakened.

By contrast, the revolutionary left leapt at every opportunity presented by the politicisation accompanying Syriza's rise; however, they remained clear eyed about the intense pressure mounted by the Troika and the Greek capitalist class that was pulling the moderate wing dominating Syriza toward compromise. While there will always be differences of emphasis among the different groups, the revolutionary left prepared politically for the inevitable crunch by being open in their criticisms when Tsipras or Syriza compromised with the lenders in negotiations or made other concessions in government (such as when they formed a coalition with ANEL).

DEBATES ON THE INTERNATIONAL LEFT

The rapid reconfiguration of the political forces after the economic crisis showed that radical ideas could find a mass audience among workers. The collapse in support for the historic social democratic parties was referred to as 'Pasokification' because Pasok's vote fell to 4.7 percent in the 2015 election.

Readers encountering these articles after Bernie Sanders' US presidential election campaigns, Podemos' Spanish coalition government and the rise and fall of Jeremy Corbyn in Britain might find the excitement generated by Syriza winning the election politically naive. Anyone on the left who expected it to deliver on its program of reversing austerity by winning the election soon realised their naivety.

Many champions of Syriza on the international left had little to say about Syriza's betrayal. Some, such as Slavoj Žižek and the late Leo Panitch, apologised for it, even lauding compromise as the maturity that comes with the responsibility of government. But most moved on to boosting the next iteration of a left electoral project touting socialism. For the disciples of Corbyn or Sanders, the intense pressure brought to bear on Syriza and an analysis of its capitulation should have been instructive. Instead, the Syriza experience was shelved without further comment.

This is unfortunate, because it provided an important test of what a broad left party could achieve. Several revolutionary organisations in the early 2000s had supported such parties as a substitute for building an explicitly revolutionary party, arguing that they could attract mass forces disillusioned with the existing social democratic parties. The popularity of Podemos in Spain in 2014, La France Insoumise and Syriza's electoral breakthrough are evidence for this.

However, another argument was that, in building these projects alongside left reformists, the historic divide between revolutionaries and reformists was secondary to the immediate question of defending working-class living standards. There was pressure to downplay the differences between revolutionaries and reformists in parties in which the revolutionary left participated, leading some revolutionaries to liquidate their organisations. The example of how Syriza's right wing defeated the left 'from the inside' demonstrates that the old divisions permeate every struggle.

The experience of Internationalist Workers' Left (Diethnistiki Ergatiki Aristera; DEA), which joined Syriza when it formed, is a positive example of how revolutionaries can relate to these formations without liquidating their revolutionary politics. DEA members continued to produce and sell their newspaper, to identify as revolutionaries, to hold DEA events and to try to recruit people within Syriza to their organisation. Most importantly, they availed themselves of the freedom to criticise the party, which enabled them to lay the basis for a coherent explanation of the capitulation when it came. The DEA's two elected representatives played a pivotal role in cohering opposition to the new memorandum and were the first Syriza members to vote against it when it was put to the parliament.

Others on the left favoured participation in Antarsya as a left alternative to Syriza. It was sometimes argued that Syriza was more electoralist than Antarsya, but both were set up as electoral fronts. The difference was that Syriza was electorally successful, while Antarsya remained electorally irrelevant. Many of us on the international left argued – at least after 2012, when it was clear that Syriza was a contender for government – that revolutionaries should vote for the coalition to put it to the test, rather than counterpose another broad left electoral front to it in circumstances where the revolutionary left was not big enough to pose its own explicitly revolutionary alternative.

An argument could be made that revolutionaries could find an audience for their ideas either outside Syriza or inside Antarsya. There were Trotskyists who pursued both options. As it was, no organisation grew substantially enough to fundamentally alter the balance of forces on the far left. This does not indicate that there was a more favourable audience for revolutionaries elsewhere.

The expectation that Syriza would be put to the test at the next election did not make it easy for revolutionary groups to grow between 2012 and 2015. When Syriza's victory sharply posed new questions, the tragic denouement came all too soon and without the sustained struggle that would have offered the best terrain for revolutionary organisations.

Supporting the slogan 'a government of the left' in relation to Syriza's election reflects, in hindsight, the difficulties the far left found themselves in with Syriza's dominance. It echoed the Comintern policies of the workers' government in circumstances when, as Antonis Davanellos of DEA has noted, the puny size of the revolutionary left was incomparable to the German Communist Party when the Social Democrats proposed a coalition in March 1920. The revolutionary left supported it in Greece because there was no way to bypass the reality: Syriza would need to be elected to be tested. They hoped that Syriza in power would sharpen social conflict, which it did. However, the struggle never came close to replicating the situation the Comintern parties faced in the early 1920s in Europe.

ENDURING RELEVANCE

The opening of a more favourable political situation for revolutionary socialists after the global financial crisis did not make things straightforward. Most of our organisations around the world are marginal, not large enough to set a political course that evades the question of how to deal with larger, left-wing reformist forces when they arise. Drawing lessons from the experience of the revolutionary left in Syriza is illuminating.

While the situation inside Greece helps to explain why struggles did not radically revive and deepen immediately after Syriza was elected, there are other examples that suggest a broader limitation. Soon after the defeat in Greece, the Labour Party in Britain elected Jeremy Corbyn as leader – a dramatic left-wing takeover of a neoliberal, pro-war behemoth. This ignited the enthusiasm of many who resented Labour's right-wing shift; a record 400,000 new members joined the party. Nonetheless, it did not revive the class struggle from its historically low ebb. Support for left-wing electoral projects is an expression of profound disaffection with the status quo, and a shift leftward can widen the audience for socialists. However, while confidence and self-organisation among the working class remains low, it is a substitute for, rather than an instigator of, the class struggle.

The wave of uprisings that crashed through Sudan, Iraq, Lebanon, Chile, Hong Kong and Myanmar in 2019–20 showed a refreshing return to combative struggle from below. Those groups faced different obstacles. However, because politics and economics cannot easily be separated, the question of how to orient to the capitalist state will be raised again and again within movements aimed at changing society. New socialist cadres will need to understand the limitations of the 'pink tide' governments in Latin America and the fate of left parties like Syriza if they are to navigate future upturns in struggle.

The European ruling classes exacted their price for years of profits by bankers and corporations: the Greek working class plunged into misery; pensioners had to support their adult children's families; the exodus of young people without jobs; the suicides; the unkempt streets. The resistance of all those caught in the crisis inspired us, but their leaders, in Alexis Tsipras and the moderate left politics – echoes of Stalinised Marxism – that dominated Syriza were not worthy of it. The job of socialists is to learn what we can from each defeat to forge something worthy and lasting.

DISPATCHES FROM GREECE 2015

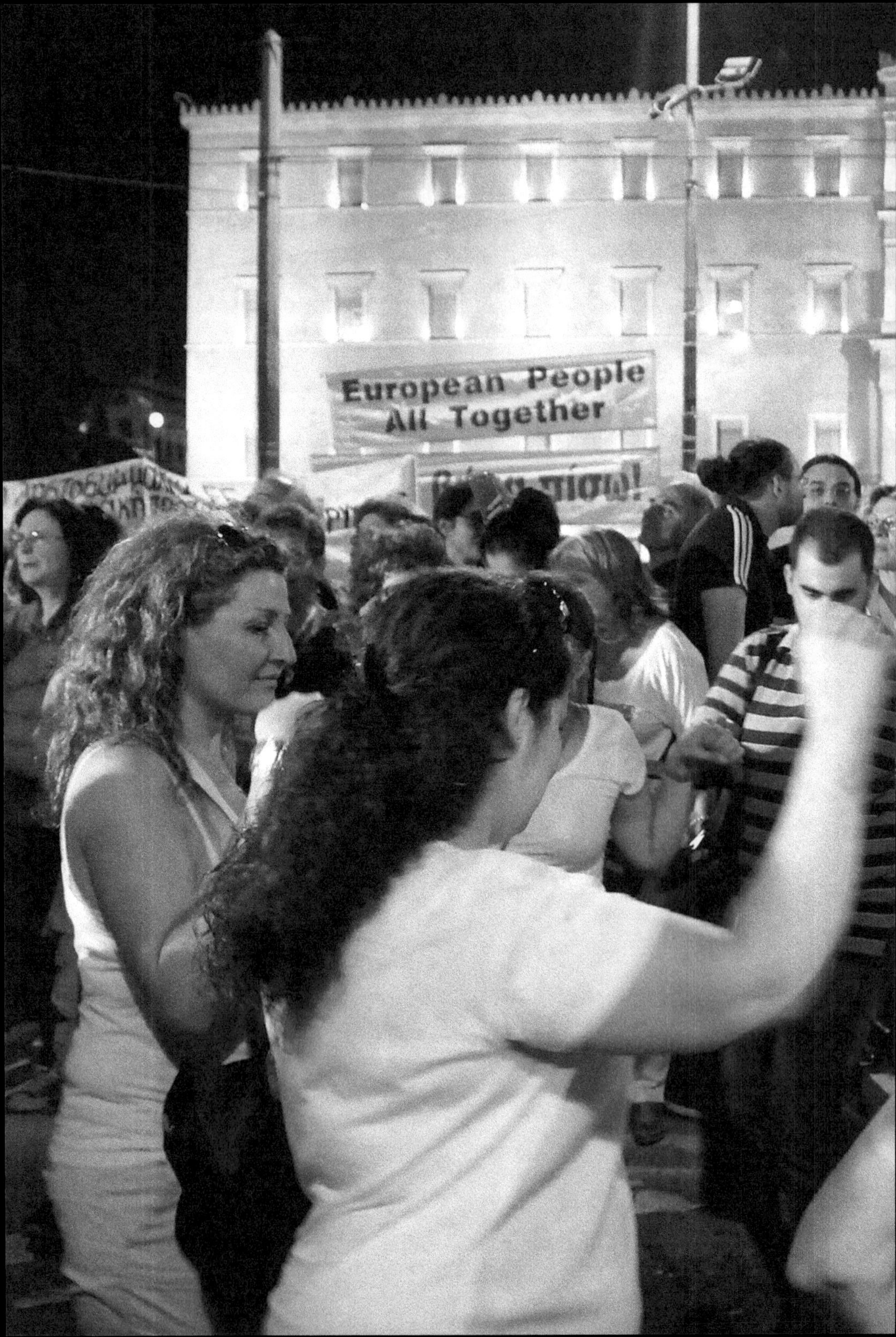
European People
All Together

BREAKING ALL THE RULES
01 JULY, WEDNESDAY

Alexis Tsipras' announcement in the early hours of 27 June that he would call a referendum for Sunday 5 July on the deal proposed by the EU institutions has broken all the rules. Prime ministers rarely ask the people who elected them what they think. Negotiations over matters of finance and state are conducted by ministers and the heads of banks in fine hotels. But for one week, these matters will unfold principally in the streets, cafes and workplaces of Greece.

In Syntagma Square Monday night, tens of thousands came to a rally initiated but not formally called by Syriza. Many attendees wanted to make it clear that this was a question of democracy. 'This should have been done not only now, but five years ago,' said Steven, a student who, like many there, was not a member of Syriza but had voted for them. 'Our families and our friends have suffered a lot from pension cuts and job cuts and after five years, this program hasn't done anything.'

Four years earlier, the same spot where we were talking had been thick with tear gas as riot police battered 50,000 people who were trying to stop the vote on the first memorandum. Alexis carried the placard last night that he'd made for that earlier demonstration. It said: 'Our dreams are what keep us awake' – a reference to the slogan 'We are awake', raised in Athens in response to the Indignados movement in Spain, which had asked the people of Europe: 'Are you awake?' It was a call to follow their example and spread the occupations.

Today it is the Greek example that everybody is watching. Everyone I spoke to at the rally was acutely aware of the significance of the referendum for Europe. Fokionas, a young member of Syriza, said he is open to a deal, but not the one on offer. What Europe's rulers fear, he said, are not the financial but the political consequences of a Greek rejection. He was conscious of how a 'no' vote will affect the elections in Spain in September, or people in Portugal, Ireland and perhaps even Italy. 'What they are so afraid of is a new rising of the people of Europe,' he said.

This is exactly what has driven the intransigence of the Troika since February. As columnists question whether the Eurogroup pushed Greece too far, we should recall German Chancellor Angela Merkel's warning to Greek voters in January. She said that if they voted in a government that refused to pay the debt, they would get no succour from the rest of Europe. From the beginning, the Troika has wanted to teach the Greek people a lesson that would be marked in Barcelona, Dublin and Turin – there is no alternative to austerity.

The European ruling classes so far this century have headed off challenges to their vision of normalcy under 21st century capitalism: the traditional parties of left and right being thrown into turmoil, the Indignados, protests of hundreds of thousands and general strikes in Greece. The establishment is used to getting its way, which is why the rich are mortified by the prospect that waiters, taxi drivers and cleaners could bring that to an end. That is what is at stake on 5 July.

If the tone of European Commission President Jean-Claude Juncker at his press conference yesterday reflects the desperation of a ruling class in crisis, Merkel's much sterner appearance reminds us that they will use every weapon at their disposal. They have the media and the parties of the right inside Greece campaigning vigorously for a 'yes' vote. Crucially, the European

Central Bank's decision to end the ELA, the lending instrument meant to be available to ensure the solvency of Eurogroup members' banking systems, was designed to inflict maximum chaos in the lead-up to Sunday.

The Greek Government's response – closing the banks and the share market for a week and limiting withdrawals at ATMs – was a vital countermeasure against a bank run and the acceleration of capital flight. If the vote were to take place in an atmosphere of panic, it would be much more favourable to Europe's rulers. It also points to how it is possible to impose democratic control over the banking system, usually presented as operating according to the autonomous laws of the market. Some branches reportedly will open to allow only pensioners, some of whom don't have cash cards or know how to use an ATM, to make withdrawals.

The decision to allow people to access cash to go about their lives, but to stop investors from shifting millions to overseas accounts, shows that there need not be a separation of politics and economics. The government has also announced that public transport will be free all week. The union covering doctors has said there will be no charge for examinations. These are practical ways of demonstrating what an alternative to austerity would look like.

Do not doubt that Tsipras means to win the referendum. As people gathered in Syntagma Square, he gave an interview reiterating that his government could not implement the measures in the draft agreement of 26 June. However, he also said that a strong 'no' vote would strengthen his hand in the negotiations. This is at odds with the position of many on the left within and outside of Syriza, who say that a deal is impossible when all that is being negotiated is the extent of the austerity Greece must bear.

The referendum is more than just a vote. It is a social mobilisation of left and right, of class. It is also more than just acceptance or rejection of a particular draft agreement. The question of austerity itself is at stake.

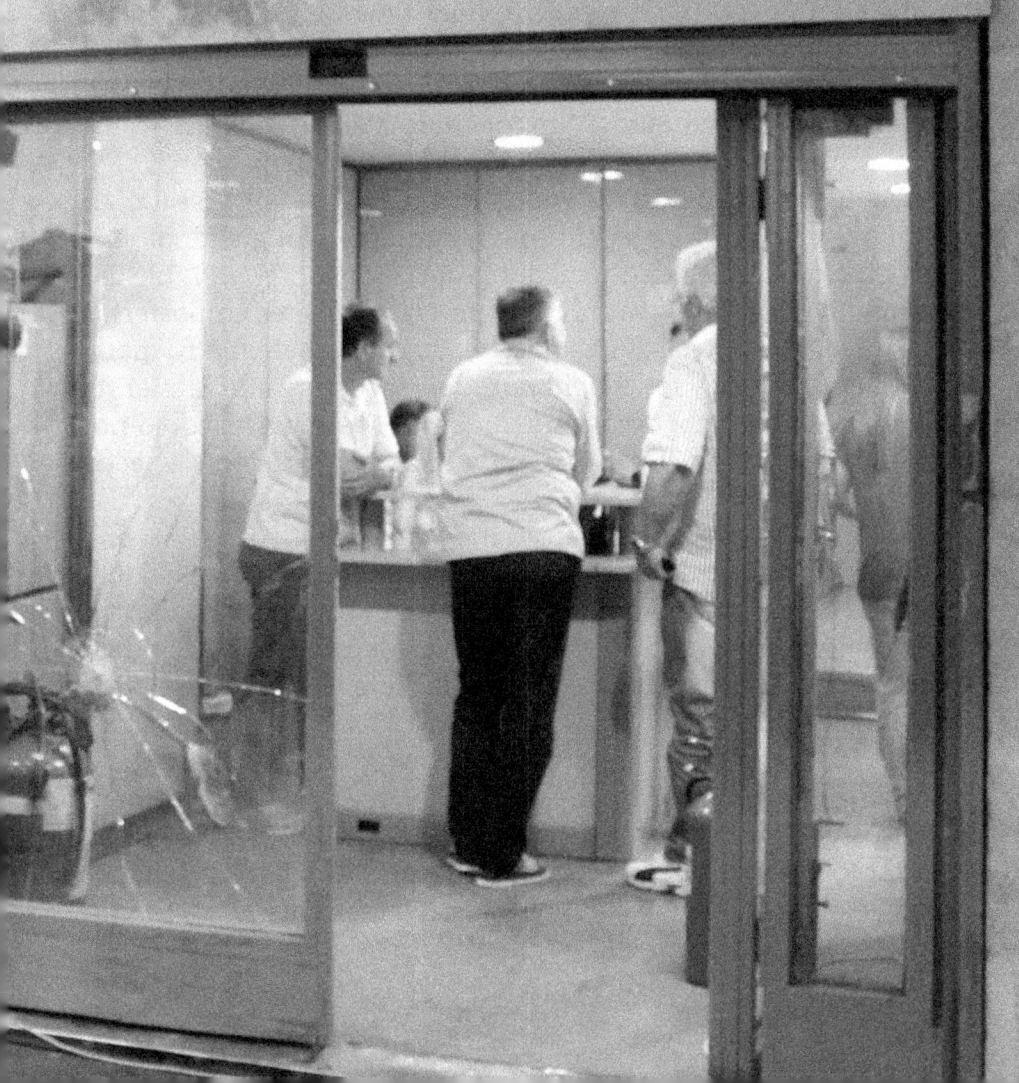
ΧΑΡ. ΤΡΙΚΟΥΠΗ 50

'NOTHING IS NORMAL'
03 JULY, FRIDAY

Setting out from my Athens hostel yesterday under threat of yet another thunderstorm – this was the third in the three days – I asked the cleaner if this was normal for Greece at this time of year. 'No,' she said. 'Nothing is normal in Greece at the moment.'

It is impossible to forecast events beyond hours, let alone days. Wednesday was a perfect example. While the Eurogroup and Greek Government met, rumours flew around that a deal would be reached if Prime Minister Alexis Tsipras either cancelled Sunday's referendum or campaigned for a 'yes' vote (to accept the demands of the Eurogroup for more austerity). Some in his own ministry publicly and privately urged him to do so.

The Communist Party – which has taken the ultra-sectarian position of calling for abstention on Sunday – along with others, was quick to issue a denunciation. Most waited, though this did not mean idleness. Street poles were being covered in posters. I recognised the official Syriza posters, but there were many, many more. Preparations for neighbourhood meetings and leafleting of the cafes and streets continued apace. The activists could not afford to lose an hour, but everyone hung on for Tsipras' speech clarifying what was going on.

When it came, comrades from the Red Network in Syriza, one of the two factions that make up the Left Platform, were palpably relieved: there was no deal. The referendum will go ahead and, because the Eurogroup's position has hardened, there will be no talks before Sunday. The status quo, if there is such a thing this week, prevails.

The Eurogroup has determined its way forward, but there is division – a sign of the depth of the crisis. French President François Hollande reportedly urged an immediate agreement so as not to risk an 'OXI' win (Greek for 'no'). German Chancellor Angela Merkel and Eurogroup President Jeroen Dijsselbloem said

there would be no talks until after the referendum. In a game during which both sides have gambled the house, the most powerful player at the table, Merkel, has put all the chips on getting a 'yes' vote on Sunday and bringing down the Syriza government.

In recent history, the European ruling classes have not had to deal with a popular left reformist government that includes significant sections of the far left. They thought they could bring Tsipras to heel in the usual ways and that, in office, he would see how things are done. He gave them every reason to think that would work. But in the end, they did not give him something that either the left of the party would back or that the right of the party could sell to the bruised population. Now, he must go so that order as they know it can be restored.

There are enormous forces arrayed against the government and the working class that stands behind it. The parties of austerity – New Democracy, Pasok (the Social Democrats) and To Potami (liberals) – the organisations responsible for a 'yes' rally on Tuesday night, are the local representatives of the European bourgeoisie's campaign. Alone, they would not be sufficient to secure the 'yes' victory in the poll. Pasok is spent, decimated in terms of members, voting base and control of unions, because it implemented the first memorandum. To Potami is a creation of the media and was anti-austerity on a populist basis before the election but pro-agreement at any cost since. New Democracy, the traditional party of big business, is still powerful, but it is not a mass organisation. That limits its ability to mobilise.

However, they are aided by every media outlet campaigning for a 'yes' vote. Employers in the private sector are trying to wreak havoc by standing people down without pay, telling them they can't do business while the banks are shut and to blame the government for that. One even tweeted on Tuesday that he would be distributing workers' wages that night in Syntagma Square only to those who showed up to the 'yes' rally. Both the local and European bourgeoisie campaigning for a 'yes' vote have made this about Grexit – Greece leaving the euro currency. In that context, Tsipras and Finance Minister Yanis Varoufakis' argument that Greece can stop the austerity but stay in the euro area is a delusion.

They have taken this framework into the negotiations since January. However, as the *Guardian* has reported, the IMF's modelling shows that, even on the most optimistic projections, Greece will be mired in debt for another decade at least. Greek economic growth is not the objective of Europe's rulers. Crushing working-class living standards and opposition to neoliberalism is the goal.

Tsipras and Varoufakis want a 'no' vote in the referendum and a deal on Monday or Tuesday. The contradiction is that, while Varoufakis says: 'Vote "no" to help us reach an agreement and stay in the euro', most people are voting 'no' to austerity – which will continue under any agreement signed with the Eurogroup. We will know how this contradiction plays out only if the 'no' campaign wins.

The main question in people's minds now is what will happen if Greece exits the euro area. People in the street are not blind to the fact that this is a looming possibility as early as Monday. But the government's refusal to talk about it blindsides the people who want that question answered.

One of the key divisions in Syriza, between the Left Platform and the party majority that backs Tsipras, is that the left has an answer to that question. 'If we are forced out,' they say:

> we will have a chance to implement the Syriza program – liveable social security, affordable public transport, housing for the homeless, collective bargaining, raising the minimum wage, a moratorium on people having their utilities cut off because they cannot afford to pay their bill and much more.

In the context of an exit, when bank stability will be crucial, the demand to nationalise the banks would be posed concretely.

Similarly, the demand to nationalise pharmaceutical companies to ensure people can still get medicine would take on a tangible dimension. Nationalisation is not the same as workers' control – for now, these are political questions posed by the impasse rather than by workers' own activity.

There is an extraordinary amount of work to do. Thousands of people have put everything in their lives aside to do it. Bands of activists are leafleting the streets constantly now. The last I encountered was a group of four German comrades who, like me, only knew one word of Greek and on the strength of that booked their flights to join the struggle.

As I write in a cafe, there are groups of middle-aged men drinking coffee and interrupting each other in earnest argument. They have been at it for hours. I catch a few words, 'fascists', 'anti-fascists', 'Tsipras' and 'democracy'. They are not musing about the weather. The college opposite is covered with banners. Activists tell me the politicisation now is wider and more intense than at any time in the last five years.

A comrade pointed out last night that the Greek people have been told many times that the country will be plunged into mayhem if they don't accept the austerity. The first and second time, they were prepared to hunker down and accept it. However, this is a repeat of that show, and they feel they've already seen that episode numerous times. Time now for something new.

BATTLE LINES
04 JULY, SATURDAY

Syntagma was the story on Friday night. Liza, a hospital worker, was ebullient: 'I've been to many demonstrations, and this is the best one ever'. Like many, she was not a member of Syriza or any other left organisation. The sense of having suffered so long for no progress under the Troika's memorandums drew more than 150,000 people to the square in central Athens. They came to say 'OXI' – no. People were crammed into feeder streets seven blocks away. It dwarfed the 'NEI' (yes) rally, held at the same time, by at least five to one.

This rally matched or was bigger than any in the last five years because there is a great feeling that everything people have sacrificed and struggled against since 2010 is on the line. There is a tremendous feeling here that history is being made by pensioners, the unemployed, students and workers.

The 'OXI' campaign gathered in squares around Greece. Courage, dignity and resistance were the watchwords. Musicians played songs from the civil war era all night in Syntagma. The crowd sang along. I did not know their history well enough to know why some songs were better known than others. But I recognised 'Bella Ciao', the anthem of Italian resistance to fascism, and joined in the crowd's exuberant rendition. They sang to draw strength from the working-class tradition of resistance, especially during the civil war, and because the same battle lines are drawn today.

This is a battle between two contending classes; those still wavering will be won to one side or another.

The 'NEI' campaign comprises the European ruling classes and the Greek ruling class (embodied by the Hellenic Chamber of Commerce), which are unleashing economic chaos throughout the country. The European Central Bank (ECB) has stopped Greece's access to Target2, the mechanism that allows ease of international business transactions for goods between euro area members. The ECB has also said, by way of bribe, that it will restore the emergency lending almost immediately on Monday if Greece votes 'yes'.

The department that supervises labour law compliance has taken hundreds of calls from workers who report that their bosses have said they will be fired on Monday if they vote 'no'. There is a report today in the *Financial Times* – immediately denied by the Greek Central Banking Authority – that the government will

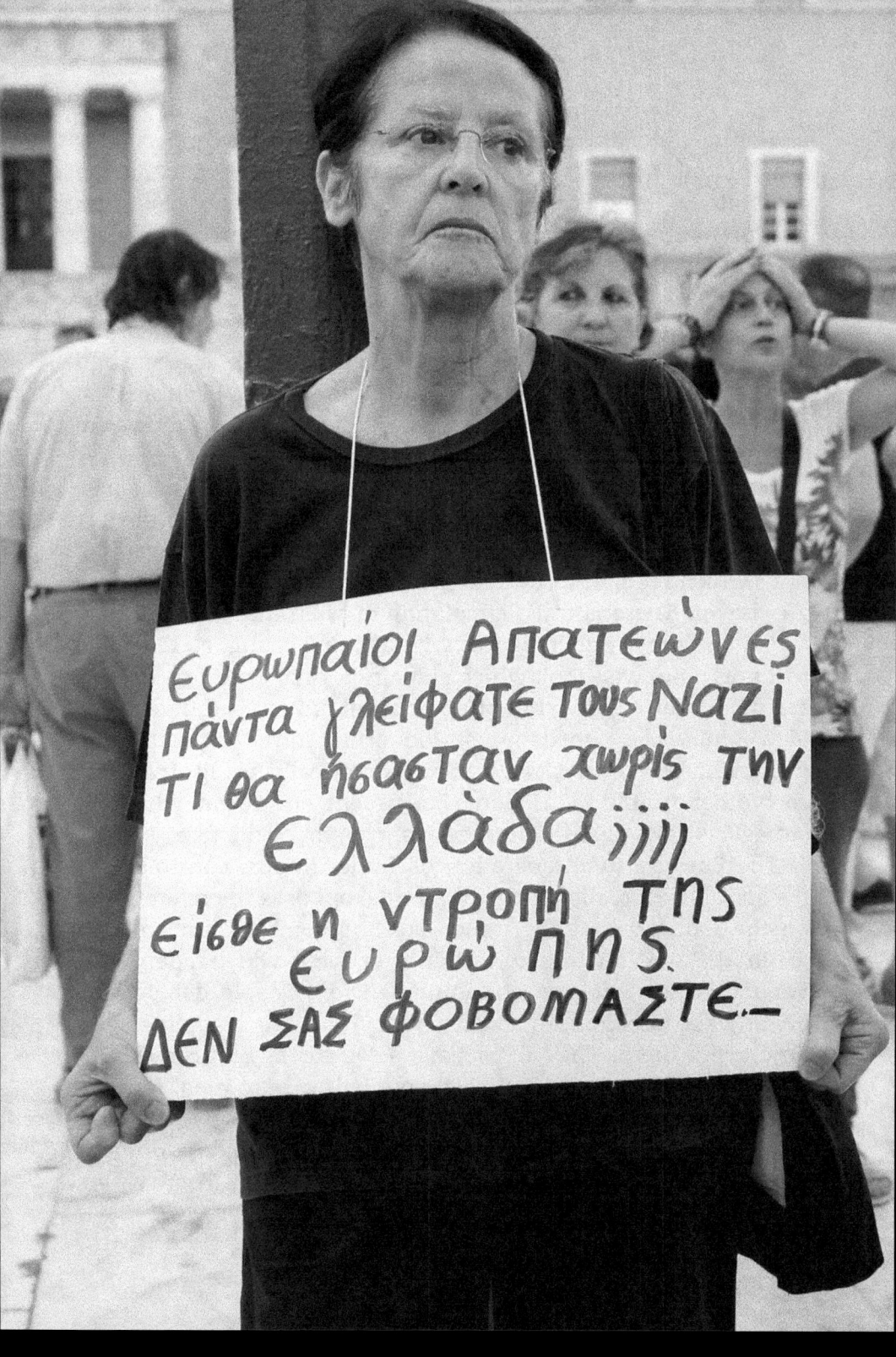

seize one-third of deposits over €8,000. Most workers' savings ran out long ago. This is aimed at the middle classes. It comes in a climate of grossly overstated but repeated reports of shortages in supermarkets and rumours that the banks will run out of notes after the weekend.

The 'yes' campaign is also backed by the social democratic parties of Europe, the Greek parties of austerity (Pasok, To Potami and New Democracy), the Greek liberal middle classes and fascist-inclined middle classes and the media establishment in Greece and across Europe. Can you imagine a more powerful enemy than these forces all combined?

There is no in between or middle ground: lifestyle magazines, arts organisations, the Bar Association, former prime ministers and economists come out daily for 'NEI', showing that organisations which seem innocuous are not neutral when the battle lines are drawn. There is a list circulating of well-known musicians, actors and other public figures who are supporting 'NEI'. People will not forget who took which side. In normal times, class lines are more blurred; division often appears only as a difference of viewpoints. The two demonstrations in central Athens Friday night, which were physically and metaphorically facing off against each other around the Hellenic Parliament, show that, when the struggle is at its peak, class once again comes to the fore.

The European Confederation of Trade Unions, controlled by the social democratic parties of Europe, opposes the referendum on the grounds that the issues are 'too complex' for workers to understand. But the uncertainty of what will happen after Sunday is not a failure of comprehension. People debate eloquently the problems that exist today and are grappling with how to fix them. They don't have a Master of Economics. But they can tell me that when they entered the euro area, farmers who'd made a good living growing tobacco or corn were told that they could no longer do so. Why? Because it would be done in other countries that had bargained for the contract. The workers were not given an alternative. Their livelihoods were destroyed, and now they cannot understand why Greece imports the products they once grew.

The crowd roared with scorn at the mention of Sky or Mega Channel – the big capitalist TV stations. Occasionally during the week, the voices of 'OXI' hijacked their microphones. In a vox pop of pensioners, a Sky reporter shoved out of shot a frail, old man who, when asked how he was affected by the restrictions on bank withdrawals, said: 'It does not matter about me. What matters is that people are resisting'.

The biased coverage has not caught people off guard. They recall that it was the same in the lead-up to the elections in January. People showed then that they were no fools. My taxi driver tells me: 'All the drivers will vote "no", all the rich will vote "yes". The media say we are lazy. I work 14 hours a day. It is the rich who are lazy'. It is a view shaped from life experience, and it won't be shifted by a news anchor or commentator with a PhD in economics.

It is remarkable how calm people are in the face of all the threats and economic sabotage. People are both full of hope that change is possible but, at the same time, braced for things to get worse before they get better. Maria, a physiotherapist, tells me: 'Voting "no" is the only way our lives will be better. Not now, but in 20 years, for our children'.

If the poll were conducted in workplaces, the 'OXI' vote would be overwhelming. However, among the middle classes, older people and in regional areas, which are traditionally conservative and where the left's reach is weak, the right's terrorisation has greater purchase.

The numbers rallying in Athens on Friday are a powerful projection of the left's strength – which can sway those who are wavering. The other strategy is to demonstrate that there is an alternative to the economic mayhem of the bosses. Panagiotis Lafazanis, the minister for production and reorganisation and a leader of the Left Platform in Syriza, in February prevented the

shutdown of the sugar industry. Thousands of workers and farmers depend on this industry.

This week, according to one comrade I spoke to, thousands of homes had their utilities reconnected. The bakery cafe in which I now sit is giving people who need it free bread. In these ways, the government and its supporters can show in practice how it is possible to use Greece's resources to counter the bosses' offensive. Such measures can be extended to every part of the economy, starting with the areas where shortages could develop, such as in pharmaceuticals and gas. The owner of Mega Channel, for example, is also the owner of the main toll road into Athens, which takes €1 million per day in cash. If cash reserves run low, the people will be well served by the maxim, 'follow the money'.

For now, the involvement of workers who have the power to take such actions is on the level of debate only. That debate will sharpen considerably within days if 'OXI' wins. In theory, workers always have the power to seize control of production and use it to meet their needs. We know that it takes confidence and organisation to realise that potential – but almost everywhere, our side has been lacking in both and unable to exercise that power in a long time. If 'OXI' wins tomorrow, it will give the labour movement across Greece a surge of both.

OXI OXI OXI

Going into battle, you are never assured of victory. At such times, everyone is accountable for their positions and their actions. Whatever the arguments about the ins and outs of every group's tactics, most of the left have campaigned as if they are locked in an existential battle. The Communist Party (Kommounistikó Kómma Elládas; KKE), however, has written its death warrant with the call to abstain from the vote. It has instructed people to download and print the party's own ballot papers, which say 'OXI' to both the draft agreement of 26 June and another memorandum. It argues that the 'yes' and 'no' votes are the same because Tsipras will keep negotiating. It says that the referendum is 'fake' and 'blackmail'. These ballots will be void.

KKE members were not in Syntagma on Friday with the more than 150,000 mainly working-class people, some of whom were former members. One of these was the mother of the man who acted as my impromptu translator during speeches and songs. She sang the old songs with gusto. She had given her youth to the party and had watched its death agony since the rise of Syriza, which the KKE has denounced as a false messiah. In doing so, it treated the workers whose hopes Syriza raised as irredeemably deluded.

The KKE held its own rally on Thursday night. About 10,000 attended. It is down from the rally of 30,000 in January, when the party refused to call for a vote for Syriza in the national election. The decline in numbers is an indication that many of its own members will defy the leaders and vote 'no'. However, 10,000 is not an irrelevant number of people, especially when many are militants of long standing and organised in key industries such as the waterfront. Given that the vote hangs in the balance, there will be a reckoning if 'OXI' loses.

There will also be a debate within Syriza about the impact of emphasising that a 'no' vote will enable Tsipras to cut a deal. He has been saying it all week, but he did not say it in his speech to the rally last night. It is at odds with what people believe 'OXI' to be about – a gateway to a better future out of the rut of austerity. For now, this is not the most important thing. In spite of the huge concessions Tsipras offered as late as Tuesday – which will be put back onto the table even if 'OXI' wins – the crowd in Syntagma was waiting expectantly for hours to hear Tsipras speak. Their roar when he appeared rocked the square.

This does not mean people will accept everything he does. It does not mean that everyone has forgotten the concessions. But until Sunday at least, that takes second place. That is a reality that revolutionaries have to calibrate into their strategy, whether we like it or not. The KKE epitomises the dead end of denunciation from the sidelines. We ought to remember the old builders' labourers' slogan: 'If you don't fight, you lose'. Greek workers and the Greek left have given tremendous battle. If the worst happens on Sunday, they will take stock, soberly and with heavy hearts, but not for long.

OXI OXI OXI

People who spend their lives fighting for a better world are inclined toward optimism, attuned as we are to seeing in every flicker of resistance a glimmer of how things could change. For the Greek working class, it is a matter of survival. Here, I have learned a new meaning of the term 'lost generation', which often is used to designate those long-term unemployed young people who came of age just as the crisis hit. Men in their mid-30s and older told me that one of the sacrifices they had had to make was putting off starting families. It reminded me of the lines from Bob Dylan's *'Masters of war'*, a song about the Vietnam war that does just as well for the class war in Greece:

> You've thrown the worst fear
> That can ever be hurled
> Fear to bring children
> Into the world
> For threatening my baby
> Unborn and unnamed
> You ain't worth the blood
> That runs in your veins.

There is a poster plastered around Athens of German Finance Minister Wolfgang Schäuble's face. The picture was taken when he was informed of the referendum. Schäuble had likened voting 'no' to committing suicide. In fact, 11,000 people are estimated to have taken just that course because of the austerity. The poster's slogan, which is in reference to this, roughly translates: 'He's been sucking our blood for five years'. 'OXI' means no to more blood spilled for debt. It means no to the bloodsuckers. And it is the no that will stop the blood cold in their veins.

A HISTORIC VOTE, BUT CHALLENGES AHEAD
06 JULY, MONDAY

It is the morning after the biggest celebration Greece has seen since the fall of military rule. An emphatic 61 percent of people voted 'OXI' in the country's referendum on whether to accept European-enforced austerity. People gathered in Syntagma Square in central Athens and in squares around the country. Families celebrated together in their lounge rooms with neighbours. Friends came together in bars. This was more than a party. It was a social convulsion after five years of bitter austerity.

In calling the referendum, Prime Minister Alexis Tsipras unleashed a social outpouring. It was a tactic, after five months of negotiations, born in the space between the reactionary right of the Eurogroup and the radical left of his own party, which threatened to vote against any more compromises. If anyone had doubts about its significance, they only had to see the photos of people celebrating to understand what it meant to have won. There were tears in the eyes of old men as comrades and friends embraced.

I soaked up every glorious minute. Coming out of the cafe where I had been ensconced reading the results, I immediately ran into an impromptu demonstration of a few hundred heading toward Panepistimiou station. They were mostly young people;

quite a few, like me, had come from across Europe to campaign. Cars tooted, and drivers and marchers together whooped with joy. They were chanting about pointing their faces in a new direction of struggle and resistance.

At the gathering point for Syriza members, music was playing. As we neared, they broke into 'Bella Ciao', the song of the Italian anti-fascist resistance. People had been singing it in Syntagma on Friday night at a massive 'OXI' campaign rally. Tonight, people were dancing as well. All week, there had been rallies in Syntagma. Twenty thousand 'OXI' supporters on Monday night. Similar numbers on Tuesday for the 'NEI' campaign. On Thursday, the Communist Party had its smaller outing. Then, on Friday, a history-making final 'OXI' campaign rally of several hundred thousand, dwarfing the 'NEI' rally on the other side of the parliament in Olympic stadium.

There were probably thousands of meetings and events in other areas of Athens and across the country, but Syntagma had been the focus. Everyone knew that the winner would be here on Sunday. People stood as victors at the top of the stairs in front of the parliament and watched others stream into the square. The fountain in the centre was illuminated by red lights. Mothers grasped onto their adult sons, swaying together as they sang songs from the civil war era.

The sense that this was their night was profound. 'What has happened here is something unique,' said one man that I interviewed on the way to Syntagma. 'One and a half parties – Syriza and [its coalition partner, the Independent Greeks] ANEL against all the world. Against the media, against the system – the European system and the Greek system. Everybody was against us and we almost died but we say "no".'

The European heads of state and the leaders of European social democracy all said: 'Vote yes'. Not only did they say it, but they used their control of the media to make every news anchor, journalist and entertainer a mouthpiece for the 'yes' case. News reports ran exaggerated pieces about shortages in supermarkets. Rumours that bank deposits would be seized on Monday were spread to create panic. They conducted push polls that made the 'yes' camp appear stronger than it was.

The ECB's decision to end Emergency Liquidity Assistance a week before the referendum transformed it from creditor to blackmailer. Bosses stood down workers without pay, blaming Syriza for closing the banks. Others threatened that workers would not have a job to come back to on Monday if they voted 'no'. It was nothing short of terrorisation. But, as one voter said: 'It has not just been chaos this week; it has been chaos for five years'. This sentiment underpinned people's resolve.

'Germany has made three wars against us and this is the worst,' said the taxi driver taking me on election day to a polling station in Nikaia, near the port. He echoed what I had heard all week: people were tired of being dictated to by German Chancellor Angela Merkel and her Finance Minister, Wolfgang Schäuble; a war had been unleashed against them, robbing them of democracy and dignity.

At the polling station, a voter supporting her elderly mother stood in the blaring sun. 'This is Nikaia. We know what it means to stand up to Germany and the Nazi,' she told me. During the Nazi occupation, the men of Nikaia were lined up in the square while collaborators, wearing masks, identified resistance fighters to be executed. Grandparents still remember the atrocities. They have told their children these stories, who have in turn told their children.

This history of refusing to submit in the face of the most horrific brutality is colliding all the time with the present. This week, the legitimacy of capitalist institutions was undermined. The organisations of civil society that are able to prop up capitalist rule by appearing reasonable and independent all vigorously campaigned for a 'yes' vote. These are the collaborators, and a people at war will not readily forget their faces.

The two areas I visited on polling day had 'no' votes of more than 70 percent, higher than the national average of 61 percent. It was breathtaking watching the results roll in. Our side was much stronger than the polls had predicted. People now are riding high from their triumph over the immense political and economic forces arrayed against them. The masses have asserted themselves, and they know it. They know that Merkel had a plan to deliver more economic misery. They know now that they will be an example to others. They know that their own struggle

will be strengthened by its spread. As one man told me: 'We can't do this on our own. I hope all European peoples will rise up'. When my translator friend, George, struck up a conversation with a young Sevillian, he wished them the same success in the elections in September.

However, Tsipras' strategy is not to use the 'no' vote to begin the necessary social reconstruction promised when Syriza won office in January: to raise the minimum wage and social security, restore collective bargaining, reconnect the utilities in homes, spend money on public housing, health care and education etc. Instead, he has said the 'no' vote will enable him to go back to Brussels to negotiate a new agreement.

Many of the Eurogroup finance ministers, however, appear firm that there should not be much, if any, compromise on their part. Granting debt forgiveness or easing austerity, some of them reason, would send a message to the workers in Portugal, Spain and beyond that if you elect a left government, you can at the very least renegotiate with the European institutions. They fear a contagion of democracy that could mean many billions of euros sacrificed to the popular will.

It may be that the position of Schäuble and his lieutenant, the leader of the Social Democratic Party of Germany, Sigmar Gabriel, wins out. They say that the EU should cut its losses, stop putting up with the impertinent Greeks and their crazy ideas of democracy, boot them out and hope they go hungry. That is the example they hope to set. It is not a new thought. Timothy Geithner, former US treasury secretary, in his 2014 book *Stress test: reflections on financial crises*, recalled the attitude of the European finance ministers during a 2010 G7 meeting in Canada: 'We're going to teach the Greeks a lesson...we're going to crush them'.

However, Sunday's result adds risk to this position. It will further expose the fact that they do not give a damn about the wishes of the majority. That could confirm what many workers across Europe already feel: there is no real democracy. The European ruling classes can ill afford people's cynicism becoming open defiance.

Furthermore, a Grexit, whatever the trigger, will deepen the economic crisis in the country. That will require immediate and decisive actions by the Greek Government, which also could serve as a counter example to neoliberal normalcy – one that inspires hope, rather than fear, in workers across the continent. A statement by the Internationalist Workers' Left, a leading force in the Left Platform inside Syriza, spells some of this out:

> We understand the pressures and dilemmas faced by the government, and in particular the extortion tactics of the creditors with their threats to the banking

system. Those threats can only be answered by the nationalisation of banks and the establishment of public control, under the direction of the workers in this sector. This is decisive for the functioning of the whole economy. The 'no' vote was an unwavering demand for the reversal of austerity. It is a call for Syriza to decisively implement the program of the radical left, taking all economic, political and financial measures necessary.

There are many potential scenarios, and, as we watch how it unfolds, we will do well to remember that the decisions that will be made in the coming days and weeks are being made by people who are still scrambling to understand the real meaning of Sunday's result.

The main weakness on our side is that Tsipras showed, in the middle of the referendum campaign, that almost everything was on the table in the negotiations with the country's creditors. If Tsipras comes home to Athens from Brussels with an agreement in his briefcase, we will soon learn the answers to the major questions of the day: to what extent are the European ruling classes willing to compromise to keep Greece in the euro area, and what sort of compromise will the left within Syriza accept and vote for in parliament?

The debate will be most intense within the party. However, it will be carried out in the context of a mass politicisation brought on by the crisis, heightened through many confrontations, intensified this week and mediated by some assessment on the left of what people 'on the street' will accept.

I am tempered by the taxi driver who said to me on Sunday that the people had elected Syriza to do 10 things but expect them to do only two. He was critical of that, but it was also a measure of what, for him, would suffice for now, given the circumstances. Despite compromises, Tsipras is more popular than ever because he is perceived to have stood up to the creditors' demands.

Even if a compromise is reached, there are still possibilities. If workers can stand up to a historic campaign of fear waged by the European establishment, they might begin to stand up to the daily tyrannies of their petty managers.

In a hospital this morning, people were talking about the referendum. Someone came up with the idea that they could surround the mayoral building in the city until the mayor, who had spoken at 'yes' rallies, resigns. The idea had spread around the traps by 9.00 am. It is a sign of the way people are now thinking.

On Sunday night, Panayiotis, a journalist in his mid-30s and previously a member of Antarsya, an anti-capitalist coalition outside of Syriza, turned to me in a crowded bar and said: 'Tonight we are free'. It is freedom from being dictated to by capital for a week – but there is also a resolute sense that the crisis will not end tomorrow.

One man told an ABC radio journalist: 'We are hungry today, we will be hungry tomorrow. But today we stood up and said "no"'. He was expressing pride in resistance, but also pragmatism about what can be achieved without a much greater level of struggle.

Some among the Left Platform within Syriza are not opposed to a deal per se. They share Tsipras' framework that the struggle unleashed during the referendum is a means to a better deal. Tsipras was emphasising at the huge 'OXI' rally on Friday, even before the referendum had been won, that from Monday Greece must rebuild national unity. He then called a meeting of the leaders of the discredited pro-austerity parties this morning to build consensus for reaching a deal.

The radical left will probably find itself in a smaller minority than before the referendum, when there was little that could be salvaged from the worse and worse offers the Troika put on the table. How much of a minority will probably depend on the shape of the agreement – if one can be reached, that is. If there's no agreement in a few days, and the strangulation continues, the questions of how to organise society to meet people's immediate needs will be pressing.

The class schism that was torn open last week is one of the best legacies of the ongoing process. The sense of 'us versus them' is palpable and clarifying. In a very short week, there has been a reckoning. Over the coming months, we will learn the full measure of Sunday's victory in the preparedness of workers, students and the unemployed within Greece and across Europe to continue the fight against every manifestation of austerity.

RUPTURES
12 JULY, SUNDAY

In the early hours of Friday morning, Alexis Tsipras won the consent of the Hellenic Parliament to pay off the blackmailers. He gave up the pensioners. He gave up the public servants still with jobs. He gave up the people who will not be able to afford food and coffee when the value-added tax (VAT) is increased to 23 percent. He has given in. And when he did, he gave up the 61 percent of the population who resoundingly voted 'no' to an agreement that arguably is better than what he has now proposed.

German Chancellor Angela Merkel and European Commission President Jean-Claude Juncker were livid after the 'no' vote. They moved to tighten the strangulation of the Greek banking system and threaten Grexit – to punish the Greek people and to increase the pressure on Tsipras to buckle. It worked. Yet it is not clear that the European establishment will accept a Greek surrender. German Finance Minister Wolfgang Schäuble has called for a 'time out', a temporary Grexit.

In a speech to parliament on Friday night, Tsipras argued that his proposal delivered on his mandate to make an agreement to stay in the euro currency zone. 'I never asked the public for a 'no' vote to mean a Grexit or rupture,' he said. However, for millions of people, 'no' was a vote against austerity. A majority clearly do want to stay with the euro. But the question is, at what cost?

The fear of Grexit is real. If it transpires, the banking crisis will come to a head quickly and cripple the everyday functioning of society. There is an alternative, articulated by the Left Platform of Syriza and the far left outside of the party. Measures such as nationalising the banks and taking control of key industries could ensure stability and meet immediate human needs. However, no preparations have been made to this end. Tsipras' insistence for the last five months that it is not an option has contributed to the fear, which is well founded, that Grexit would bring chaos. It also means that a Grexit would be more chaotic than would otherwise have been the case.

Just as class polarisation underpinned the polarisation between the 'yes' and 'no' votes last week, there is a second distillation along class lines within the 'no' vote. When I asked people on Friday what they thought of Tsipras' proposed agreement, they shook their heads, grim and bewildered.

The woman who makes me a different kind of coffee every morning had wondered the day before why the Europeans were leaving Greece to rot, refusing to agree to debt relief. On Friday morning, I suggested that they might because Tsipras had agreed to the terms that they demanded. She was not relieved, but embittered. If the VAT rises, she said, all the shops still open in her street would close. 'We work 12 to 14 hours a day. How can they ask us for more?'

In Chalandri, an area described by a comrade as 'the new Manhattan' (borne out, it seemed to me, by the young affluent people in the bar at which I ate lunch), interviewing people on the street near a bank, I encountered uncertainty about what was the worst option. A few had voted 'yes', and they thought Tsipras had failed because he could have made a better agreement if he had surrendered back in March. They will start to feel more confident out of this. Among those who voted 'no', there was a bitterness that, whatever happened, life would be a struggle, and the system is rigged for the rich.

I returned to Keratsini, a working-class area near the port. I had been here at one of the polling booths last Sunday. In this area, more than 70 percent voted 'no'. There was a resoluteness in people's responses that I had not come across elsewhere. A young delivery driver, hanging out with some mates at the coffee franchise, forcefully told me that it is better to leave Europe than live under the conditions being demanded. He is no economist, he said, and his mates weren't political. But as we were talking, one of his 'apolitical' mates said that we need a revolution.

Panos, who works in the shipping industry, said Tsipras' proposal 'is to turn a something into a nothing. I don't know what it is – capitalism, they...' He trails off. It's something I hear a lot from people who know the crisis was the making of the corrupt old parties and the creditor Troika of the European Commission, the ECB and the International Monetary Fund.

Panos considers himself lucky because he has a job, even though it pays half what it used to. Nevertheless, it is a struggle for his children. It is another scorching summer day. He is on an enforced holiday because his employer has said that the company can't pay people for July. Before all of this, he would be at the beach, drinking with mates and relaxing. But that is unthinkable now – not because it is particularly costly, but because no one lives like that when they are anxious about their future.

The strong sentiment here is an echo of the tremendous defiance of the people who voted 'no' last weekend. We will never know precisely what portion of the 'no' voters are like the working-class people I spoke with in Keratsini. But we can say that, when people stood up to the enormous intimidation of the media, their bosses and the Troika last week, they showed tremendous resolve.

Tsipras and the vast majority of Syriza MPs have not shown the same courage. It is much more disorienting for the people who voted 'no' to be betrayed in the night by their own generals than to be defeated fighting the enemy. There is no excuse worthy of the working-class people who showed such defiance on Sunday.

However, sentiment can dissipate quickly if it is not harnessed into organisation. People disoriented by their 'no' being turned into a 'yes' need to hear that there are others like them who do not want another agreement. If there is no big expression of opposition, they probably will feel alone and abandoned.

In the coming days, people will look for the opposition within the left of Syriza. Stavroulla is a member of Syriza in Keratsini. She is 'shocked' and 'very bitter' about the proposal: 'I think this is a big mistake. There are other ways and Syriza cannot agree that there's only one alternative.' With tears in her eyes, she said: 'This goes against people's vote'.

If the leftists within Syriza stick by the 'red lines' that the party promised not to cross, they can show that people's resistance last week and in the general strikes and battles with riot police over the last years do not amount to nothing. That will be the basis to reconstitute a left that fights the implementation of austerity. The two MPs, Ioanna Gaitani and Elena Psarea, from the Red Network, which is grouped around the revolutionaries in the Internationalist Workers' Left, voted 'no' in the parliamentary debate on Friday night. That was a clear stand on a fundamental question: yes or no to more austerity. According to Syriza central committee member Stathis Kouvelakis:

> Seven MPs of the Left Platform abstained, including its two most prominent ministers (Panagiotis Lafazanis and Dimitris Stratoulis)... Among them Marxist economist Costas Lapavitsas and Stathis Leoutsakos, member of the political secretariat of Syriza. The four ministers will resign in the next few days. Fifteen other MPs of the Left Platform...issued a statement explaining they will vote 'yes' in order not to deprive the government of its majority at that stage, reject the proposed agreement as yet another austerity package and warn that they will not vote for any signed agreement that includes austerity when it comes to parliament.

These numbers are disappointing because it is not the strongest base from which to organise opposition. But the debate is just beginning. There is much speculation that, because Tsipras was forced to rely on opposition votes for support, the government has been destabilised. This has been used by Tsipras to increase pressure on the left in Syriza to not break ranks. It had the desired effect on Friday night. However, it will make things difficult for him as the individual laws for pension reforms, public service cuts and the other austerity measures come before the parliament. It has also established that there is a minority opposition around which rank-and-file members of Syriza can coalesce.

The editorial in today's edition of *Avgi*, the party paper, calls for a new election to be held soon. This would allow Tsipras to increase his majority and would discipline those MPs who abstained. Elections would force a debate in the party, which would be expressed in the district nominations and potential disendorsement of MPs who refuse to hand out official party propaganda pushing the Tsipras line. It would be the most intensely politicised election held since the beginning of the crisis, coming on the back of the huge social mobilisation for the 'no' vote and at a time when Syriza is at a crossroads.

Alternatively, the German hardliners will win the day and push through some sort of temporary exit. In such circumstances, the demands the left have articulated with more force over the last few weeks – for bank nationalisation and other measures to prevent shortages – will be prescient. Tsipras may be forced to carry out the left's proposals to address the social crisis.

One sign of the volatility: a group of men in their 30s or 40s – a truckie, a muso, a security guard and a waiter – drinking wine guffaw that last week they were supporting Tsipras and now they're supporting Schäuble. They want the drachma back. More seriously, they say Tsipras has been a disappointment to the 61 percent who voted, they thought, against another memorandum.

It is impossible to predict what will happen in the next 48

hours, but the last 48 hours has posed a new set of tasks for the left. People who voted against austerity have watched as their victory has been turned into its opposite. Tsipras has used his prestige to force through another agreement. Building opposition to the passage of a new memorandum is urgent. If a clear stand is not taken by the left, all will be lost in the din. Right now, people are straining to hear that an alternative is still possible.

THE LEFT RESPONDS
14 JULY, TUESDAY

The deal Alexis Tsipras has done with the European establishment will put money into the pockets of the corrupt oligarchy, rather than food into the mouths of pensioners and the unemployed. The hope that people put in him just over a week ago is not a debt that can be deferred. He defaulted on the Greek working class when he refused to leave the table during the 17-hour Euro Summit negotiation that ended in total capitulation.

Tsipras, two weeks ago, tried to break a negotiation deadlock with the European establishment by calling a referendum on austerity. He could have used the historic 'no' vote to build something. But he didn't fight. That exposed to the rulers of Europe the reality that the Syriza leadership would agree to anything to keep Greece in the euro area.

Europe, led by Germany, turned the screws. This was the most punitive action in the history of the European Union. It was not about economics. It was about humiliating everyone who stood against austerity. The EU elite determined then that regime change was necessary. And they have got it. Syriza, as a party of the left, is almost certainly dead. This is the endpoint of a strategy based on a fatal underestimation of the opponent.

Europe is not a democratic community of peoples. It is a dictatorship of private and state creditors in which those with the most skin in the game dictate the terms and care little for reason or suffering. Theirs is neoliberal Europe. Nothing else. No clever argument, no brilliant game theory of former Finance Minister Yanis Varoufakis, is capable of blocking their agenda.

Class struggle is the only thing that can stop them.

There is shock and disbelief in the workplaces and coffee houses. Only a week ago, people were dancing with joy in the streets. Now they are told, because of their resistance and defiance, that they will be saddled with something worse than what they rejected.

There is a call from the federation of public sector unions for a general strike on Wednesday, before the parliamentary vote on the new memorandum. This is an opportunity to build a fightback out of a setback. The initiative has come from the anti-capitalist left.

The political earthquake that annihilated New Democracy and Pasok in January is taking its time to be felt at the top of the sclerotic trade union bureaucracy. META – Syriza's trade union faction – and the radical left have grown in influence in the unions. But the old leaders remain. In a meeting on Monday, raging argument from radical left speakers from the floor butted up against a line of cantankerous old-man bureaucrats who occasionally lost their temper. When it became clear that the left was going to win the vote, with the begrudging support of the Communist Party and Pasok, the activists started filing out, back to work to organise or to union meetings across the city.

Activists I speak to – some in Syriza, some in other groups, and some not in any group – are concerned that they do not have long enough to turn the sense of disbelief into anger. They have a matter of hours. These are the times when activists rue the gulf between what urgently needs to be done and the number of people who can do it. The Greek far left is the largest in Europe. It is impressive and committed, yet this is still an enormous task.

It is aided by something that people outside of the left and from afar can miss. While mass consciousness is struggling to

understand what has taken place, the anti-capitalist left has a framework to make sense of it. The radical left organises with the knowledge that change comes through struggle and that the state is not neutral. Its activists knew the limits of Tsipras's strategy from the beginning and, one way or another, have been preparing for this day.

They were not caught off guard. They say constantly that the struggle goes on. They are prepared to organise in whatever circumstances they find themselves in. This is why they could act quickly and decisively. Within hours of the first parliamentary vote on the new agreement on Saturday morning, they were in neighbourhoods, handing out leaflets outlining their response.

The other side of the struggle is the debate going on at every level in Syriza. Two members of the Red Network, the left in the party's Left Platform, on Saturday morning voted against a new memorandum. They gave a clear lead to every Syriza MP and to the party rank and file looking for an alternative.

As I write, the parliamentary fraction of the Left Platform is meeting to discuss the betrayal on which they must pass judgement on Wednesday. It is much worse than what they either voted for, spoke against or abstained from on Saturday. Their stance on Saturday fell well short of what was required. But opposition has hardened since then; and most, if not all, are expected to vote against Tsipras' deal. The question is how many Tsipras will lose from the party majority.

He cannot say that he didn't know whom he was dealing with. He once called them a 'gang of thieves'. When a member of one gang joins a rival, he is put through an initiation, to test if he can really be trusted. Typically, it will involve making him go after his former friends. So Syriza MPs who vote against the memorandum should brace themselves for expulsion and an acknowledgment that that project is over. But voting 'no' will be a clarion call to workers who are looking for a lead. It will be the first step to reconstituting the radical left.

The ensuing debate in the party will determine how many of the 30,000 members can be drawn out of the current fog. The party is relatively new, is a creature of the radical left and has as its base many thousands of activists who joined because they wanted to fight austerity. That means that there are many to fight for. It was a good sign that the youth wing of the party had a presence at an anti-memorandum rally in Syntagma Square on Monday night. I spoke to one of their members, Konstantinos, who was grappling with Syriza's whole strategy and what the MPs should do:

> It seems now that this strategy that said, 'Let's go easy with the EU' has been proved to be wrong… I think that the agreement that we're bringing is worse than the previous two that the others [Pasok and New Democracy] brought. The European Union have shown their real faces. They are really hard neoliberals who won't be afraid to show what they're made of if they get pressure. I wouldn't like to be a Syriza MP right now… I don't really know what I would do, but I think they should probably vote 'no' and lead the country into a general election.

There are still many arguments to be won at all levels of the party. The Red Network has called for the party organs to be convoked so that these debates can be had out at every level. It is a minority within the Left Platform, but well placed, having built up credibility with party members.

This is what happens when there is a serious engagement in debates on the left: people remember the positions different groups held and can test their utility in the struggle. Many of those in the party who said in February that it was too early to criticise Tsipras see now why it was necessary. The outcome of the debates will determine whether or not Greece ends up with a radical left that is the sum of its existing parts, or one that is a pole for those, within and outside of Syriza, who want to carry through the mandate of the referendum.

Many have said that, in succumbing to German Chancellor Angela Merkel and the EU establishment, Tsipras has overturned the stunning victory of 'OXI'. But that victory showed that millions want an end to austerity and are determined to resist immense intimidation to fight for it. Their defiance and struggle offer the reference point for a new left, armed with the lessons of the last five years of austerity, the last five months of left government and the concentrated learning of the turmoil and betrayals of the last two weeks.

NEW BATTLE LINES
17 JULY, FRIDAY

The post-referendum political turmoil has reset the political situation in Greece. On one hand, the betrayal of the 61 percent who voted against the 26 June draft agreement has undone the pre-referendum momentum. The working class again has been demobilised.

On the other, the beleaguered Tsipras now faces a revolt inside Syriza – precisely the situation he called the referendum to avoid. The mutiny began last weekend, when two MPs, Ioanna Gaitani and Elena Psarea from the Red Network in the party's Left Platform, voted against giving the prime minister the authority to broker a capitulation to the country's creditors. More than half-a-dozen others abstained, including parliamentary speaker Zoe Konstantopoulou. By doing so, they laid down the gauntlet; from there, opposition hardened among Left Platform MPs.

When it came to the decisive vote on Wednesday night, the question was not whether more of the 25 Left Platform MPs would vote against the memorandum, but how many Tsipras would lose from the party majority. The Left Platformers were joined by Yanis Varoufakis, who denounced the agreement as akin to the Treaty of Versailles, and Konstantopoulou, whose strident speech will have shaken the party core and was heard in lounge rooms across the country. Varoufakis and Konstantopoulou are the most well-known party MPs other than Tsipras, and popular in their own right.

I spoke to Gaitani, a member of revolutionary group the Internationalist Workers' Left, at a rally in Syntagma Square before the vote on Wednesday. '"No" from the left means that there is a left, and that there will be a left tomorrow that will reject the memorandum of austerity,' she said. 'There are many within the left that are hard for this position. They give the hope that there is still a significant part of the left that does not support austerity... We need to gather as many forces as possible around an alternative political platform so we [can] go on to fight against austerity in Greece.'

A statement of opposition signed by 109 of the 201 members of Syriza's central committee was published hours before the parliamentary vote. It illustrates the depth of opposition at every level of the party:

> The agreement with the 'institutions' was the result of the blackmailing of the country through economic strangulation. It is a new memorandum, with onerous and humiliating terms of supervision, disastrous for the country and our people. We realise that suffocating pressure was put on the Greek side in the negotiations, but nevertheless, we believe that the people's proud no vote in the referendum must forbid the government from succumbing to the extortionate ultimatums of the creditors. This agreement is not compatible with the ideas and the principles of the left. But most importantly, it is not compatible with the needs of the working class and the popular masses. This proposal cannot be accepted by the members and the cadres of Syriza.

Similar statements were passed unanimously or by large majorities of the district coordinating committees, which were convened to register members' opposition to the memorandum.

The revolt is strongest in these levels of the party.

In the parliament, Tsipras made a final pitch for the agreement. He acknowledged that more austerity will be recessionary. Konstantopoulou declared that it will cause 'social genocide'. Tsipras appealed to Syriza MPs not to let the creditors and the political right in Greece bring down the government. This argument is a real pressure on MPs who do not want to see the right get back into office. Yet the logic of that argument now seems flawed. A Red Network statement said:

> This new memorandum essentially and practically
> overthrows the government led by Syriza:
> programmatically, but also politically, since it transforms
> Syriza into an austerity government with an increasingly
> pro-austerity composition.

In the parliamentary debate, even the pro-austerity forces goaded Tsipras. New Democracy leader Evangelos Meimarakis rhetorically asked why Syriza had for so long attacked his party for implementing previous memorandums, when Tsipras now was asking the parliament to support the worst deal ever. There was no doubt that the agreement would pass, but it is politically damaging for Tsipras to rely on the neoliberal New Democracy and Pasok for votes.

The political establishment has been shaken by the fact that Syriza is not the sort of reformist party we are all used to. Social democracy today champions neoliberalism with hardly a whimper of opposition from any of its sections. By contrast, Syriza is rooted in the struggles against austerity and has drawn in people with a track record of standing up for their principles. One example is Deputy Finance Minister Nadia Valavani. She was jailed under the military regime that ruled Greece from 1967 to 1974 and spent five months in solitary confinement for her activities in the Communist Youth Organisation. She voted no to Tsipras' betrayal and has resigned her post.

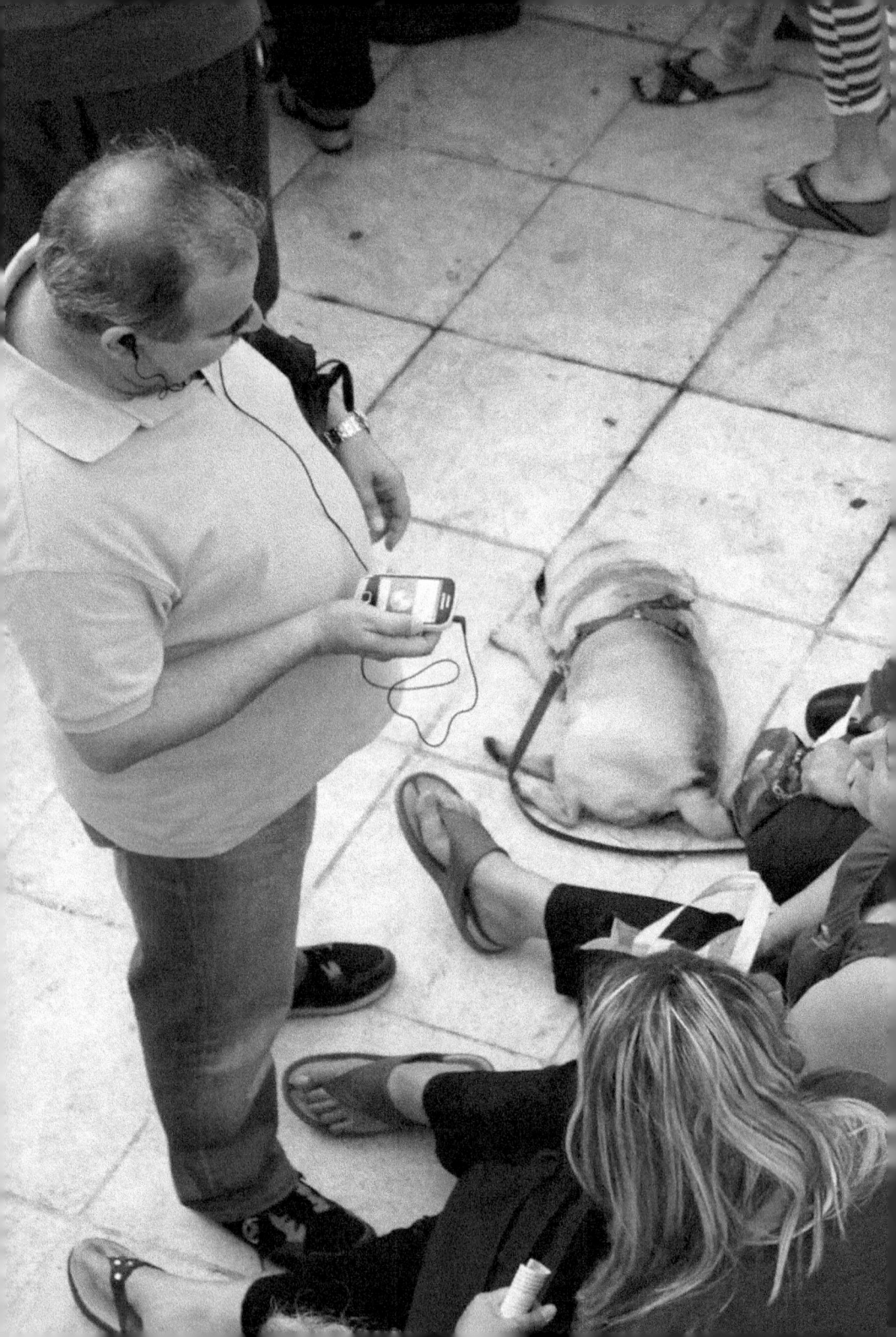

German Chancellor Angela Merkel is unlikely to trust the government to implement the agreement until it has been cleansed of its left wing. But Syriza does not have an apparatus with a proven record of disciplining the left and clamping down on opposition. There is a hard-right section that called for the left to be expelled, and there will almost certainly be a cabinet reshuffle to remove Left Platform dissidents. However, it's unclear at this stage how far Tsipras can go without further inflaming the opposition.

OXI OXI OXI

Syriza's failure stems from its flawed strategy of negotiation, of believing that the eurozone leaders could be reasoned with, of being unwilling to mobilise the power of the working class and of left illusions in the European project. This is a failure of reformist politics – the politics that has dominated the party since its inception. But it still needs to be distinguished from old social democracy in order to grasp the scale of the opposition now brewing.

Revolutionaries within Syriza are not surprised by what has transpired. For years, they have been pursuing arguments about how the party should position itself to fight austerity. For example, the Red Network opposed the coalition with right-wing nationalists, the Independent Greeks, who all voted for the latest agreement.

It was incredibly important that the revolutionaries didn't water down their politics or get caught up in the Tsipras cheerleading that took hold as the party gained strength and took office. Thousands of party activists who previously supported Tsipras's strategy are now grappling with why it failed; they want to resist the party leadership. More people now are open to the arguments about what to do next. The Red Network has pledged to fight for the party's soul. A section of the Left Platform is cohering the opposition and, in the process, is drawing lessons. That could be the basis for a regrouping of all those within and outside of Syriza who will fight the implementation of the new measures.

The federation of public sector unions called a strike on Wednesday to coincide with the vote. It is unclear how widely the strike was observed, but militants I spoke to in the teachers' union and municipality workers' union estimate that it was a relatively low turnout on this occasion. That was not surprising. Among the mass of workers, there can be a feeling of resignation. Tsipras has undermined the confidence that people gained from the referendum victory. Nonetheless, there recently have been strikes around specific issues, including by the dock workers of Piraeus, who shut down the port in protest at the plan to privatise it.

As MPs were debating the memorandum inside parliament, the riot police – present in great numbers – fired tear gas at thousands of protesters gathered outside. The cops chased people for kilometres. They were like vicious dogs unchained after being kept for too long on a short leash. The radical left, making up the core of the demonstration, pulled out their masks or handkerchiefs. For many, it was a routine that they had become accustomed to under the previous governments. This was the first time the government of the left had unleashed the state on them.

Both inside and outside the parliament, new lines have been drawn. However, history does not follow the same laws as a wristwatch. The defiance of the working class, demonstrated in the referendum, and the lessons drawn from this defeat will be the basis of reconfiguring a left that is stronger for having fought.

TURNING RESIGNATION INTO RESISTANCE
27 JULY, MONDAY

'A Pyrrhic victory against the Greek people' is how Alexis Tsipras described the new memorandum. It isn't yet clear that this is the case. At the conclusion of the battle of Asculum in 279 BC, King Pyrrhus of Epirus remarked: 'One more such victory and we are undone'. His army had just smashed the Romans in a struggle for control of Magna Graecia (the coastal areas of southern Italy).

Success, however, had come at great cost – several thousand of his soldiers were dead.

European leaders today are not counting their dead; they are, in fact, counting on more victories and view the strangulation of Greece as the key to their future. European Council President Donald Tusk revealed in the *Financial Times* on 18 July that the ruling classes fear that any concessions to Syriza would galvanise a left opposition in other countries also: 'I am really afraid of this ideological or political contagion, not financial contagion, of this Greek crisis,' he said:

> The febrile rhetoric from far-left leaders, coupled with high youth unemployment in several countries, could be an explosive combination. For me, the atmosphere is a little similar to the time after 1968 in Europe. I can feel, maybe not a revolutionary mood, but something like widespread impatience. When impatience becomes not an individual but a social experience of feeling, this is the introduction for revolutions.

The creditors hope that the 'Syriza example' will show that the left says one thing and, in office, does another – just like the rest of the political establishment. They hope, that, by punishing the Greek population, they will give workers across the continent the message that there is no alternative to neoliberal Europe. Yet there also is a possibility that the integrity of the European project has been undermined by the creditors' strategy. A people wounded might not lie down and die, as the rich hope. The political contagion they fear may yet result from their own obstinate strategy.

In the domestic press, the attacks on the Left Platform and the Syriza MPs who voted against the bailout have been at a hysterical pitch since the vote on 15 July. Tsipras is lauded for his 'maturity' and sense of responsibility. The corollary is the old trope that the radical left is a bunch of rebellious teenagers who speak out of turn and don't know what they're doing. The message is that governing should be left to the adults who know the right time for sacrifices and how to discipline misbehaving children.

Left Platform members who voted 'no' have been removed from their ministries. Parliamentary speaker Zoe Konstantopoulou cannot be removed because her position is meant to be independent. Tsipras has asked her to resign. The move that has provoked the most outrage from the party membership is the refusal to convene a central committee meeting. A majority of party leaders signed a statement strongly condemning the bailout, so it is in Tsipras's interest to delay any meeting. Holding off fresh elections until after the situation has 'stabilised' is also a way to defer a confrontation with the party's left.

The left is accused of trying to split the party and bring down the government. This was the basis of Tsipras's appeal to representatives in the parliamentary vote on 15 July. It was effective. Syriza MP Ioanna Gaitani reported at a Red Network meeting that the opposition within the parliamentary group is broader than the vote indicated. (The Red Network is one of the two factions within the Left Platform of Syriza.)

The pressure is also reflected in statements such as Left Platform leader Panagiotis Lafazanis', that he 'wholeheartedly' supports the government and the prime minister but opposes the memorandum. Should resistance to the memorandum mean the government falls, it will be because it followed the path of austerity, not the fault of the left, he said. The left is fighting to overturn support for the memorandum.

A second line of attack is that the Left Platform has no plan or, if it does, that it should have presented it earlier. But the Left Platform has a well-publicised plan: the Thessaloniki program. It is not a set of principles thought up in the dark ages. It was formulated last year in Greece's second largest city. It was the basis of the party's 25 January election triumph. It is Plan A, B and C.

The difference between the right/centre of the party and the left revolves around the question of how the program would be implemented. Here, the centre of the party around Tsipras insisted that it could be achieved by appealing to a Europe of democracy and fairness. The refusal to countenance an alternative when the creditors refused to budge was a fatal mistake. It is Tsipras who had no Plan B and is promising to persist with the same disastrous strategy when negotiating the next phase of the bailout.

There is a more 'sophisticated' argument, prosecuted by left intellectuals such as Leo Panitch and Slavoj Žižek, which provides a justification for Tsipras's actions. Panitch talks about the war of manoeuvre as though it is all manoeuvre and no war. The manoeuvre is within the narrow confines of four concrete walls that are in his view immovable – this is the 'balance of forces' and it is adventurist to try to shift them.

Žižek falls into the same trap. 'The true courage is not to imagine an alternative, but to accept the consequences of the fact that there is no clearly discernible alternative,' he wrote in a 20 July article in *New Statesman*. He repeated the line from the right that there will be more misery and chaos if Greece leaves the eurozone. 'The prospect of such heroic acts is thus a temptation to be resisted,' he wrote. Žižek dismisses the calls for Syriza to return to the grassroots on the grounds that it is not strong enough to displace the power of the Troika. He says the best Tsipras can do is exploit divisions at the top: again, it's all manoeuvre.

The radical professors' admiration for Syriza lies in its taking office with a radical program. But the program is secondary to taking office. Any sense of how the class struggle could change the terrain and any consideration of the impact of this disastrous capitulation is absent in these 'Marxist' defences of Tsipras.

The arguments are also carried out within Syriza. They are now between those who view a government of the left as one part of a strategy to end austerity and those who view it as an end in itself, appealing for pragmatism. This position was advanced by a member of the party's youth wing at the Democracy Rising conference: the argument that you could have both Thessaloniki and the eurozone was useful to win the election – but if one is to be sacrificed, it must be Thessaloniki rather than risk a party split and the loss of office. For these people, Tsipras is a better leader than Lafazanis because a party led by Lafazanis would not win elections. This kind of pragmatism always ends in a shabby compromise – in this case, transforming the anti-austerity soul of Syriza into the best manager of the crisis.

The problem with such pragmatism is that it is about preserving the current balance of class forces, rather than calculating how working-class forces can be augmented and the forces of reaction resisted. The forces of those in power will always be greater until the moment of their imminent overthrow.

There are some on the left, most notably the International Socialist Tendency led by the Socialist Workers' Party in Britain, who draw the old lessons about reform or revolution from Tsipras's backdown: Syriza is reformist – what we need is a revolutionary party. This is a timeless truth, but the road to a revolutionary party of some weight inside the working class is not as simple as drawing up the right program and distributing it among workers.

The new situation has posed many questions for party activists. Arguing out Tsipras' failed strategy can help cohere a wider layer of activists – both inside and outside of Syriza – around a clearer strategy to oppose austerity. Such opposition cannot yet be purely revolutionary, because most activists open to such arguments come from other left traditions, such as Eurocommunism and Stalinism. There also are many independent leftists who, for years, have been involved in the trade union movement or community organising.

This was evident at the meeting of the Red Network on 18 July and the Syriza branch meeting in the second district of Piraeus which I attended last week. The Red Network was initiated by the revolutionary Trotskyist group, DEA. There were up to 300 in attendance at the meeting. Most of those who spoke, however, were not from the DEA, but independent leftists such as John Milios (a prominent Marxist economist), trade union activists from the militant teachers' union and the not-so-militant union that covers the health sector, as well as current and former members of the Left Current, the other, bigger group in the Left Platform. Members of Antarsya, the coalition of the anti-capitalist left, were also present – a testimony to the grassroots campaign work the Red Network engages in with forces outside Syriza, which will be important in the reshaping of the left.

People spoke about their initial shock at Tsipras' capitulation. For many who had great hope in the Syriza project, the first reaction was to leave and be done with it. As one activist put it to me, before you deal with the political arguments, you have to deal with people's psychological state; such is the depth of disillusionment. However, as DEA activists argued, to walk out now cedes the ground to Tsipras.

Ioanna Gaitani told how she had received a phone call from an elderly person prior to the 11 July parliamentary vote, who asked her not to sign another Varkiza. This was the treaty that the Greek Communist Party signed with the British in 1945, which resulted in the disarmament of the resistance forces. Another speaker pointed to the example of Aris Velouchiotis, who at the time refused to lay down his arms and went back to his local area to continue the resistance. The task now is to fight for all those who are looking for an alternative and want to continue the struggle.

The relationships built through common struggle and open debate over the last decade (Syriza was founded in 2004) are the basis on which the Red Network can wield influence now. It has not been easy, especially in the period after the elections, when people thought that Tsipras' strategy had to be given a chance. But the people who are only now concluding that the 20 February agreement was a portent of what has transpired remember that

the Red Network argued against Tsipras from the beginning. The experienced leftists within Syriza will not easily find the energy to start a new project from scratch, but nor will they easily take the betrayal of what they have been fighting for these last 10 years.

Those on the international left who are still telling people to go easy on Tsipras should have heard the debate in the Keratsini council rooms at the second district of Piraeus branch meeting on Thursday. The outrage was palpable. The debate went until 1.00 am. People demanded to know why the central committee had not met. Others were angry that it was taken for granted that they would put up posters for the party – yet the only people to have a say in such a major decision are the '20 LSE [London School of Economics] advisers'.

Stavroulla was there. I had interviewed her at a nearby bus stop the day after Tsipras announced the dreadful list of austerity measures he would take to Brussels. Shaken then, she was in fighting form at the meeting. She urged people to consider that, if Syriza speaks honestly and in a radical way about Grexit and the eurozone, they will take not one step but 10 steps forward; she urged people to stand up for the Thessaloniki program.

The debate was about drawing a balance sheet of what went wrong and a serious attempt to come to grips with how to turn the party around. This will not be done by accepting that Tsipras had no alternative, but by discussing the alternative plan the left can put forward based on the lessons of the last six months.

In Keratsini, the Left Platform dominates. But the borders of the different currents are shifting; for example, the meeting was chaired by a member of 'the 53', a group that includes Finance Minister Euclid Tsakalotos and representatives who abstained in the 11 July vote. The chair spoke against accepting the memorandum.

The aim of the Left Platform is to cohere opposition beyond its ranks, as it did when it organised central committee members to sign the statement opposing the memorandum. Almost all in the meeting called for a conference of members. This is vital, because it will bring to a head the debates between the left and the right of the party. For now, the left has set itself the task of fighting for the soul of Syriza. Lafazanis has said that the differences are the party's strength; on the other hand, some in the right reportedly have said that they could lead to a 'possible divorce'. We cannot second guess at this stage how exactly this will play out. However, through these debates, much can be clarified, and the left has an opportunity to build its forces.

OXI OXI OXI

In the labour movement, we say: 'If you don't fight, you lose'. However, in the battles that really shake the ruling class, a defeat for the workers can be more severe because the rulers try to inflict a blow so devastating that it will deter people from rising again. These are the times when, having put up the fight, the people need leaders who will carry it through to the end. As the French revolutionary Saint-Just put it: 'Those who half make a revolution only dig their own graves'.

German Chancellor Merkel and her finance minister, Schäuble, engineered the memorandum to be as destructive as possible precisely because the Greek working class resisted. Alexis Tsipras gave an opening to people to mobilise when he called the referendum. In their millions, they took it and delivered a resounding 'no' to austerity. On the night of the referendum victory, people were dancing in the streets because they had momentarily stolen back the power that, in normal times, belongs to their Greek and European masters. Tsipras' culpability lies in his failure to take that resistance further.

This is not to say that the class struggle can be revived on cue. The disorientation and disillusionment within the left of Syriza is also apparent in society. For those who are disconnected from the debates about how to go forward, there is a tendency toward resignation – that Tsipras did the best he could. This is why Tsipras has maintained an approval rating above 60 percent, even after the capitulation. However, thinking this is as good as it gets is a giant step away from thinking he's a national hero, as people did on the Friday before the referendum. Consciousness is fluid.

The Greek working class has demonstrated more combativity than any other in Europe in the face of the economic crisis of the 21st century. When Syriza arrived in the 2012 elections as an anti-austerity party capable of forming government, the mass struggle subsided; many wanted to see what the parliamentary road could deliver. Locals here talk about the struggle being 'frozen'. The next phase of the struggle could involve a significant thawing if people resist the implementation of the agreement. We know that the contradictions will not go away; the bailout is unsustainable, and the cycle of cuts and negotiations and agreements will continue.

The outcome of the debates within Syriza will have a big impact on the class struggle. If the left helps the government pass austerity, it will not be able to fight its implementation on the ground. In turn, resistance on the ground could break through the 'pragmatism' of those who cannot see past the current balance of forces.

There are great difficulties in turning resignation into resistance. However, the left is stronger here than anywhere else in Europe. Tens of thousands of activists identify with some form of socialism – a politics rooted in the power of working-class struggle, rather than some leftish fad like the Greens or Podemos. The greatest difficulty is that the connection between the working class and the left is weak. However, the last five years of social crisis have led to a mass politicisation, which, during the general strikes and the referendum, exploded into mass mobilisations.

In the Red Network meeting, Eleni Portaliou, Syriza's former mayoral candidate for Athens, called for the formation of a 'social EAM'. EAM was the resistance movement led by the Communist Party to the fascist occupation during World War II and to the

British-backed government that collaborated with the fascists between 1944 and 1949. The repression after the civil war could not suppress the traditions of the left. Everyone knows that the communists liberated the country through their resistance and that a popular movement revived and brought down the military junta in 1973.

Plutarch records of Pyrrhus's victory that, when he looked around after the battle, he saw:

> as from a fountain continually flowing out of the city,
> the Roman camp was quickly and plentifully filled up
> with fresh men, not at all abating in courage for the loss
> they sustained, but even from their very anger gaining
> new force and resolution to go on with the war.

To fashion such an army is not easy. But if it can be done, like the Romans, they will be more numerous, powerful and not at all abating in courage for having suffered this defeat.

POLARISATION IN SYRIZA
10 AUGUST, MONDAY

Greek democracy is in grave danger. The IMF envoy to Athens has declared that the government's proposed cuts do not go far enough. Brussels' technocrats are taking up residence to oversee the administration of Greek political and economic life. A condition of the bailout is that no legislation can be passed without first being shown to the lenders' representatives. There is also pressure to rescind legislation passed prior to the conclusion of the bailout agreement. The Greek banking system is being kept on a tight leash.

The vilification of those who voted against the agreement has increased in intensity. Stooges of the right have initiated legal proceedings against former Finance Minister Yanis Varoufakis. *Kathimerini* newspaper published a transcript of a Varoufakis phone call during which he explained that he investigated a temporary payment system in case Greece were forced out of the eurozone. The right alleges that this amounts to treason.

Similarly, the media have sensationalised a Syriza Left Platform meeting that discussed how the government could cope with an exit from the eurozone. They report this as a nefarious 'plot' hatched by communist relics of a bygone era.

The contradiction, as others have pointed out, is that the media and the right wing accuse the left of having no practical alternative to Tsipras's capitulation while claiming that the consideration of any alternative plan is a secret conspiracy. In fact, the Left Platform has made a consistent and open argument about the need to nationalise the banks and other sections of industry.

That Varoufakis has, in a matter of weeks, gone from being an object of awe to being hounded reflects the fact that the right, so discredited after the referendum, is thriving on Tsipras' about-face on the bailout. Varoufakis explained in the phone call that German Finance Minister Wolfgang Schäuble's real aim in negotiations with Greece was to impose discipline on the rest of the continent:

> He believes there has to be some fiscal transfers; some degree of political union. He believes that for that political union to work without federation, without the legitimacy that a properly elected federal parliament can render, can bestow upon an executive, it will have to be done in a very disciplinary way. And he said explicitly to me that a Grexit is going to equip him with sufficient bargaining, sufficient terrorising power in order to impose upon the French that which Paris has been resisting. And what is that? A degree of transfer of budget making powers from Paris to Brussels.

To a casual observer, Tsipras might appear to have been completely transformed – from fiery orator, when addressing hundreds of thousands of people in Syntagma Square during the referendum campaign, to a beaten man who returned from Brussels with a memorandum he said he did not believe in, and finally to a statesman typical of any other.

Tsipras was never the likely hero and saviour. The radical left always knew this. His change in posture is not so surprising, but it is nevertheless considerable. He has presided over the signing of an agreement pledging support to the Israeli military, he met the Egyptian junta leader, President Abdel Fattah el-Sisi, and he employs crass innuendo against the left. And he scored an important victory against the left at a 30 July Syriza central committee meeting. The left pushed for a party conference of the standing delegates to take place before the agreement is finally ratified at the parliamentary sitting on 18 August. Instead, the conference will take place in September, which, as Left Platform leader Panagiotis Lafazanis said in a statement published on the website Iskra, 'makes no sense, as the participants will be asked to ratify a fait accompli'.

The left had hoped to consolidate the opposition to the agreement, which was expressed earlier in a statement signed by a majority of the central committee prior to the parliamentary vote on 15 July. In the meeting, Tsipras reiterated the narrative that there was no alternative to signing the agreement, that it would be worse to have New Democracy or Pasok in office and a setback for the first government of the left to fall so soon. This appeal to prop up the government, no matter what, has traction among those for whom parliamentary manoeuvring is more critical than struggle – in this case, a group known as 'the 53', which originally was in the party majority.

There is little pressure from outside of the party being brought to bear on the waverers – it will take time for the struggle in the streets and in workplaces to regain its potency. Members of the 53 had signed the original statement of opposition but declared a moratorium on conflict within the party on the morning of 30 July. Nonetheless, in the course of the meeting,

17 central committee members resigned. All were supporters of the ex-Maoist KOE group. While the outcome of the meeting was to close off the possibility of the left winning a majority of the party, the fight is not over. The left has not been subdued. Opposition has, in fact, hardened.

The Left Current (a subgroup of the Left Platform) held a rally in a sports stadium in central Athens on 27 July. Lafazanis addressed up to 2,000 supporters. During his speech, which was punctuated by chants of 'OXI!' from the crowd, he argued that the alternative to the agreement was in the party program. Speaking of the overwhelming numbers of young people who had voted 'no' in the referendum, he recalled the youth wing of the communist-led resistance during World War II, and called on the youth to be the new generation for the 'no'.

Others who spoke included Antonis Davanellos of Syriza's Red Network; Manolis Glezos, recently retired member of the European Parliament for Syriza, famous for removing the swastika from the Acropolis during the Nazi occupation; and Petros Papakonstantinou of Antarsya, the anti-capitalist coalition. The Red Network has also held meetings in regions outside Athens, and a Left Platform event will be held in Thessaloniki soon.

The right wing has also hardened its stance. 'At the moment there are two different strategies competing in the same party: one that wants Greece inside the euro and the other that wants Greece outside the euro', government spokesperson Olga Gerovasili told reporters after the central committee meeting. 'These two can't exist together at the government level.' After the vote, Deputy Prime Minister Yannis Dragasakis said: 'I hope that we are heading for the refoundation of a new party'.

The 18 August vote will take place after negotiations with the lenders and just two days prior to the next loan payment. It will be another showdown between the left and the majority. Tsipras might call an election, which would raise the question of who the candidates will be. He has the power to determine the list. There will also be the conference in September and the election of delegates at a district level. It is the height of the summer holidays now as people return to their families for the Assumption festival on 15 August. But flash points are not far off.

Rebuilding the struggle in the streets and workplaces is vital. A meeting of 250 activists and unionists from both the Left Platform and Antarsya was held in Athens on 28 July to establish 'No until the end committees'. The report from the meeting states:

> It is obvious to everyone that a massive resurgence of the labour–popular movement is an immediate necessity to shift political and economic developments... in order to finally reverse the memorandum.

The creation of these committees is a concrete step toward rebuilding the broader struggle. It is made possible by the cooperation between activists and revolutionaries both within and outside of Syriza. Six hundred and fifty unionists and activists have signed on to the initial call for the creation of these committees. At the meeting, activists also called a demonstration to coincide with the 18 August parliamentary vote and a demonstration at the annual trade fair in Thessaloniki in September.

But the struggle has ebbed from its heights in 2011 and 2012. Among the mass of the population, there is fear that there is no alternative to the government's agreement with the creditors – and, if there is an alternative, uncertainty about what it is. In these circumstances, the political struggle within Syriza matters. The debates between the left and right of the party are decisive to rebuilding the movement. For the last three years, the party has surged forward and greatly increased its influence within the working class. To the extent that people can bring themselves to stay engaged in politics after the capitulation, they are attuned to whether the whole party is going to go along with it.

In so politicised a society as Greece, people remember the positions of different groups – even when they do not agree with them at first. Coming from Australia, I am used to answering questions about communism in terms of whether a revolution is possible or what it may look like, etc. Here, there are many groups from the broad communist tradition. They are judged by the answers they give to the questions of today.

For example, I came across two Algerian migrants discussing the Communist Party's position of opposing austerity but maintaining membership of the eurozone. Impossible, the two agreed. Like most people I have spoken to outside of the organised left, they know the positions of the various groups and their key spokespeople. When I joined the discussion, they said that now is not like it was back in 2010 or 2011 or those times in Palestine when you had people out on the street every day. The politicisation lacks the intensity it previously had. There is five years' accumulated learning in mass consciousness, but the lessons of the left government are yet to be understood on a mass level.

The debate within Syriza and its outcome are important for distilling these lessons and setting up the next phase of the struggle on clearer political foundations. In turn, rebuilding the struggle can give confidence to left activists in the opposition of Syriza to continue to fight. These poles are not counterposed. To force a counterposition – 'all Syriza and forget the struggle', or 'all struggle and forget Syriza' – is a mistake.

THE DEAL IS DONE, BUT THE FIGHT ISN'T OVER
18 AUGUST, TUESDAY

In extraordinary circumstances, the Greek parliament has passed its third and most savage agreement with the country's creditors. It secured an €86 billion loan, which will recapitalise Greece's banks and repay existing loans to the same institutions advancing the new loan. The Greek people will see none of it but will pay for all of it.

The Eurogroup of finance ministers approved the loan on 15 August, hours after the Greek parliamentary vote. In a press release, it praised the Syriza government for its 'swift' and 'determined' action. (Greek Prime Minister Alexis Tsipras recalled parliament at the height of the summer break.)

The agreement is a mark of shame on every Syriza MP who voted for it – they stood in the January elections on the basis that they represented a break with the pro-austerity parties. Now, they implement austerity with the votes of the discredited New Democracy and Pasok and their ally To Potami. They crossed the ultimate red line.

Parliamentary speaker Zoe Konstantopoulou fought to delay the vote as long as possible. Undaunted by the vicious and misogynist campaign against her in the media, and now openly coming from Syriza parliamentary representatives, she understands that, while the final outcome was never in dispute, every obstacle to attaining it matters.

When the roll call of parliamentary representatives was taken, 32 Syriza MPs voted 'no' and another 11 abstained. It is the biggest revolt of the three parliamentary votes taken since Tsipras secured the authority to negotiate a deal and the first time Tsipras secured fewer than 120 votes from the governing coalition, which is the threshold to avoid a confidence motion.

The 32 who voted 'no' included the 28 Left Platform MPs, former Finance Minister Yanis Varoufakis, former Deputy Finance Minister Nadia Valavani, Zoe Konstantopoulou and Rachel Makri. The abstentions came from the 53 group, which is to the left of the party majority.

Members of the 53 on the Syriza central committee, along with the Left Platform, had signed a statement of opposition to the memorandum on 15 July but then supported Tsipras' proposal to delay holding a party congress until the final vote had been taken on the memorandum. This gave him carte blanche to continue negotiations with the lenders, unimpeded by the democratic will

of the party. Their shifting position is a sign that there are forces within Syriza that the left must fight to win over to total opposition to the memorandum.

Tsipras is expected to call for a vote of confidence on 20 August. He wants to test the MPs who voted against austerity – will they give confidence to the government of the left or will they be responsible for its downfall and the triggering of fresh elections? In reality, the government of the left fell on 15 July, when the majority voted to accept the first round of measures that the creditors demanded to secure the bailout. The left must now take the same attitude to Syriza as it took to the two previous governments that imposed austerity.

However, the appeal to prop up the government is alluring for those whose aim is to secure power for people with similar ideological proclivities to their own. It was this, and the call for unity, that held sway when the majority blocked the left from convoking a party congress prior to the final parliamentary vote. It was this, and the call for unity, that held sway when the majority blocked the left from convoking a party congress prior to the final parliamentary vote. At that time it was at least theoretically possible for delegates to direct MPs on how to vote on the memorandum instead of rubber stamping it after the fact. It will now be held in September. It is also likely that elections will be held prior to the conference, making it even more redundant.

Tsipras will have the power to handpick the candidates. He has said that he cannot continue to tolerate Syriza representatives voting against the government's legislation. It is certain that he would deselect candidates of the left. Holding parliamentary elections prior to the conference also circumvents the left's ability to organise a new party and test the support of the candidates who oppose the memorandum.

Representatives of 13 left organisations within and outside Syriza released a statement just prior to the last parliamentary session calling for 'the constitution of a broad political and social nationwide movement and for the creation of committees of struggle against the new memorandum, against austerity and against the tutelage of the country'.

The signatories include Lafazanis of the Left Current and Antonis Davanellos of the Red Network – the two organisations that make up the Left Platform – as well as Spyros Sakellaropoulos and Dimitris Sarafianos, whose organisations combined make up the largest section of Antarsya, the anti-capitalist coalition. 'This is widely considered to be the first public step towards the constitution of a new political front that will regroup a large range of forces of the radical left opposing the new memorandum and the neoliberal U-turn of the Syriza government,' Syriza central committee member Stathis Kouvelakis said of the statement. The debates within Syriza now are critical to cohering as many forces as possible to join a new political front.

META, the trade union wing of Syriza, which is dominated by the left, also released a statement before the vote. 'We warn the government that workers will stand up and fight, as they have been doing in previous years. They will not allow the implementation of the new austerity measures and policies,' it said. Leadership from unions, the force at the forefront of combating the last two memorandums, will be crucial.

Tsipras is confident that he will increase his majority in fresh elections. The polls show that his popularity has increased because people believe he has done the best he could. While the agreement is widely recognised as the worst of the three, Tsipras was combative, rather than slavishly subservient, toward the country's creditors – unlike the previous two governments.

However, there are no polls that can measure the gulf between the hope he inspired when winning office on 25 January or during the 5 July referendum campaign and the begrudging consent of people who, today, are worn out from hearing that an alternative is not possible. In the winter, the full impact of the pension cuts, tax hikes and recession will bite. That is no guarantee of

resistance, only more suffering. But it is a reason for Tsipras to fear that his popularity will wane.

It is now clear that there is a red line running down the middle of Syriza between those supporting and those opposing the memorandum. Tsipras' manoeuvres are about how to force the left out of the party while coopting as many of its potential supporters as possible. The timeframe for the final showdown – always only a matter of months – has shortened to a matter of weeks, whether it is brought on by the confidence motion, elections or the party conference.

The new political front that comes out of these battles will in no way be an electoral rival to Tsipras in the short term. But its potential should not be underestimated. Tsipras certainly sees a threat. He wants to act before it has time to make its presence felt. The rise of the original Syriza was based on aligning itself to the struggles in the streets and by the unions. If a new political front does the same, then it has the potential to renew people's hope that an alternative is still possible.

THE DEFEAT OF THE LEFT, AND THE RECOMPOSITION
27 SEPTEMBER, SUNDAY

The Greek ruling party, Syriza, won a convincing victory in the national election held on 20 September, winning 144 seats, down from the 149 won on 25 January. Prime Minister Alexis Tsipras resigned last month to make way for the poll after he signed a third memorandum with the country's creditors. That agreement will deliver the harshest austerity yet experienced.

The calling of the election precipitated a significant split in Syriza, with more than two dozen rebel MPs forming Popular Unity (LAE by its Greek acronym). The new organisation also drew in 11 other organisations of the far left beyond Syriza's membership, as well as two significant factions of Antarsya, an anti-capitalist electoral front of a few thousand members. Yet it achieved a disappointing 2.9 percent of the vote – short of the 3 percent threshold required for parliamentary representation.

In contrast to the hostile reaction to Syriza's victory in January, media commentators and establishment figures across Europe are lauding Tsipras' victory as testimony to brilliant political acumen. They cannot believe their luck.

However, the abstention rate was a record 45 percent. Cynicism with all politicians runs high and will tar the entire left, not just Syriza. Tsipras' crime against the people is not only the imposition of austerity and betrayal of the party program, but destruction of the optimism that was unleashed earlier this year. Hope ran high after Syriza's election in January. There was an expectation that the new government would resist signing up to more austerity. The disappointment with its failure to deliver on that is palpable. Many people now believe that there is no alternative to capitulation and suffering.

Unlike in January, the celebrations by what remains of Syriza's active membership were confined to the official tent. Party members reportedly were singing 'Bella Ciao', the song of the Italian resistance. It had been sung by thousands in Syntagma Square on the night of the tremendous 'OXI' rally and victory celebrations on 5 July after the historic referendum to reject the blackmail of the Troika. What's to sing for now? A lament for the pensioners, for the unemployed, for the public servants whose lives will be squashed by the new 'cash for reforms' measures?

How to explain Syriza's re-election after so bitter a betrayal?

Firstly, Tsipras ran on the basis that he was the lesser evil than New Democracy. He had at least distinguished himself by standing up to the European establishment before the final backdown, as complete as it was. So there is a residual loyalty to Syriza.

Secondly, there is a deep resignation that the people's struggle was not strong enough to stand against the terrible pressure the European ruling classes brought to bear. This could be shifted only by the power people experience during struggle. But the great mass struggles of years past have receded.

Thirdly, the election was held before the new austerity measures bite, although pension cuts and the VAT increase were passed in July.

Fourthly, the timing of the election was calculated to hamper LAE's ability to build its forces and profile. The group took what it could out of Syriza, and there may well be more to come, but its base is still small. In this context, it was always going to be difficult.

Fifthly, talks between Antarsya and LAE failed to materialise into a united front for the elections. Their combined vote would have elected anti-austerity candidates. Accounting for why this unity was not forged will be part of the broader evaluations of the left's strategy and tactics.

Finally, the left could not escape the effect of the prevailing disillusionment with politics, which is a result of both Syriza's capitulation and the retreat of mass struggle. LAE might have been tarnished by association with Syriza, even though its core had fought the party leadership and split on a principled basis. However, the fact that Antarsya's vote increased by only 6,000 reflects the fact that disillusionment is broad based and doesn't plague just one section of the left.

Despite the election setback, LAE represents a significant recasting of the left and has made strides in building on the collaboration between different forces in recent struggles, most notably during the referendum campaign.

However, there were problems within LAE arising from its hasty formation as an electoral coalition without a constitution, branches or elected leadership. These were exacerbated by the actions of the dominant Stalinist faction, the Left Current. Decisions were often taken unilaterally by a small group around Panagiotis Lafazanis. This repelled activists who were wary of replicating the culture that emerged in Syriza, where decisions are made by an inner circle around the leadership. The political emphasis of LAE's campaign was also problematic. The central committee of the Internationalist Workers' Left (DEA by its Greek acronym), a revolutionary group within LAE, argues:

> Faced with the pressure from our political opponents, who argued that obedience to the European leadership is obligatory, we overemphasised support for an exit from the eurozone. At some point, this necessary part of our overall argument was singled out and raised above a more general program of organising a united class movement against austerity and an anti-capitalist program towards socialist emancipation. That was a gift to Tsipras and the mass media, who looked for every opportunity to slander us as the 'drachma left'.

The Red Network, initiated by DEA as the left within Syriza's Left Platform, has become a pole of attraction for people outside the Left Current. The network's influence has grown because people remember the arguments its members have been making since January – arguments that were not popular but which proved prescient. Since the split with Syriza, Red Network members have been able to cohere a wider layer of activists around their arguments about LAE's orientation. They have also been important in reaching out to layers beyond the ranks of the Left Platform. Their joint work, over many years, with social movement activists outside Syriza facilitated this.

The terrain of campaigning now shifts away from elections and toward resisting implementation of the agreement in workplaces and neighbourhoods. Committees of 'No until the end', established in the weeks after Tsipras signed the agreement, are important. However, the situation on the ground will be incredibly difficult, given the cynicism and despondency.

Lessons from experience are often bitter, but they are the ones that won't easily be forgotten. The experience of the government of the left – its election, strategy, capitulation and the split – is yet to be fully worked through. The debates now will be had as people and organisations draw up their balance sheets. These debates will be a necessary part of creating a political front capable of rising to the challenges of the coming period.

AUSTERITY BECOMES THE NEW REALITY

AN INTERVIEW WITH PANOS PETROU IN AUGUST 2023

Eight years after Syriza's capitulation and the attendant turmoil in Greek politics and society, Colleen Bolger caught up with Panos Petrou – a member of the Internationalist Workers' Left in Greece and editor of the organisation's newspaper, *Workers' Left* – to find out how the situation has panned out in the intervening years.

IT'S NEARLY A DECADE ON FROM 2015; WHAT'S HAPPENED IN GREEK SOCIETY AND WITH THE GREEK ECONOMY?

In terms of the national economy – in capitalist terms – Greek capitalism has relatively stabilised after the major crisis. It was stabilised on the backs of the working class after the implementation of the three memorandums of austerity. The changes that have been imposed on the ground – in terms of workers' rights and wages – have led some Greek Marxists to even talk about a new model for capitalist accumulation in Greece. Since 2010, wages have been pushed lower and lower, precarious labour has dramatically increased, and spending power has reduced. This allowed rising profitability for Greek businesses.

GDP remains below what it was before 2010, so it was not a full recovery. The stabilisation was also dependent on quantitative easing in the European Union. A deal that Tsipras signed with the creditors in 2018 postponed many debt repayments to the future. So the debt is now bigger, as a percentage of GDP, than it was before the austerity began. But it was a timeout in terms of debt repayments that allowed Greek capitalism to stabilise. And also, there was a rebound after the pandemic. The Greek rebound was among the best in the eurozone, based on sectors like tourism and other export-oriented industries. So we had a relative stabilisation, but it didn't translate into much improvement for the working class. Unemployment is lower, but wages are still below what they were in 2010.

So, austerity established a new reality, which has not been reversed even now, when there is growth. As a matter of fact, in exchange for the timeout in debt repayments, the measures that were imposed by the memorandums as supposedly temporary were officially recognised as permanent restrictions. Two constant trends serve to highlight the situation. Firstly, part-time, precarious jobs are rising as a percentage of new jobs/hirings, surpassing 50 percent. Secondly, each and every year, the wages share of GDP drops, while the profits share rises.

The situation is even worse than it used to be in public services like health care, education, civil protection, transport etc, and they are being privatised bit by bit. Since they are systemically underfunded, these sectors suffer from crippling shortages, and then private investors buy up parts of these services or take up certain functions as subcontractors, supposedly to cover the holes in the system. So, at all the levels that matter to our people, Greece is way worse than it used to be before the crisis.

The final point on the economy is that the 'timeout' for the debt repayments is over. The European Union is talking about the end of quantitative easing and the return to applying fiscal rules Europe-wide. Greece's debt repayments are due to begin in September 2024. Greek capitalism is one of the weak links in the eurozone. If the global economy goes down, the Greek economy will probably suffer, so even this stabilisation is undermined.

WHAT EFFECT HAS ALL THIS HAD ON THE POLITICAL SITUATION?

It has been a cycle of defeat, in terms of both social movements and politics. We have seen the re-establishment of the dominance of the right-wing party, New Democracy – which is the main bourgeois party – winning the elections in 2019 and again in 2023. They survived a major crisis. Back in 2015, they were discredited and in disarray. Many people thought they were done and that they would never recover. So, one aspect of what has changed since 2015 is that the main party of the capitalist class re-emerged and won a succession of political electoral victories. They are electorally dominant in the absence of a major rival.

I would not overestimate it though. We're not talking about the right wing having complete hegemony in society, but it is a very dangerous enemy. They are strong. They have benefited from the defeat and the betrayal of Syriza and its subsequent mutation. They've benefited from the stabilisation of Greek capitalism, so they have support among the middle classes and they enjoy the full backing of the ruling class for now.

They embarked on a counter-revolutionary project. 'Counter revolution' is a very strong term, because there was no revolution, but it is the agenda of a revanchist, right-wing government. When they won back power in 2019, they made it clear that they were determined to make sure that the left would never win power again in this country. That was not about Syriza winning an election in the future. It was about destroying the left – the ideas, the union strength and the left-wing culture. That was not achieved, in my view, during their first term, meaning that there still exists a vibrant far left in Greece that sustains a protest culture. Maybe there are many problems facing this far left, but it still exists. It has the capacity to mobilise a sizeable milieu of the vanguard when it matters.

During their first term, New Democracy faced many serious challenges, which led to important mass protests. So I would say we have a polarised situation, because New Democracy is strong and aggressive but we have the re-emergence of strong social movements. This polarisation was not expressed in the ballot, since our pole doesn't have a political or electoral expression to challenge New Democracy in parliament, because the major opposition parties remain in crisis.

I would categorise the situation by distinguishing two periods. Under the rule of Syriza, it was a complete situation of defeat, meaning there were no struggles whatsoever. We could hardly mobilise anyone beyond the hard core of organised members of the left. Things rebounded after New Democracy took power and, importantly, in the past couple of years. I would say that the protest movements are putting an end to the period of defeat in the social field. But, on the political field, the radical left has still not recovered from the political defeat.

WHAT HAS HAPPENED TO SYRIZA SINCE 2015?

That's actually part of the explanation for the dominance of New Democracy in electoral terms. Syriza, after 2015, has been accelerating its mutation as a social–liberal, centre-left party, like most of the European Social Democrats. Their rule was a typical capitalist rule when in power, and it's telling that it was not just applying the measures dictated by the deal they signed with the creditors. It was about becoming a party of governance, as they always wanted to be, in all fields, meaning racist policies on the border, nationalist policies in the competition with Turkey. In these fields of policy, there was no fig leaf excuse like, 'the creditors forced us to do it'. They became a typical party, fit to rule Greek capitalism in every field, and this was accelerated while they were in power.

There was an ideological mutation, reflected in their speech, meaning that the narrative of Tsipras gradually shifted from 'this is not our program', which was what he argued in July and August 2015. He started talking more and more like a typical bourgeois politician, meaning that he spoke of the need for private investments and argued that we need reforms to bring investors and growth. At some point, they adopted the creditors' program as their own.

Whatever is left that resembles a left opposition inside Syriza, they maintain that the party should never adopt the program as its own. They say we could accept the program imposed on us, but it's not ours. This was their last line of defence, facing a leadership that started taking pride in its achievements in 2015–19. Organisationally, you cannot describe Syriza as a party, at least not as a left-wing party. By that, I mean that it all revolved around the personality of Tsipras, while party structures – from top to bottom – stopped functioning.

At some point, while in opposition to New Democracy, Tsipras was re-elected as Syriza's leader, by a vote of non-members (unless we consider as 'member' anyone who pays two euros and registers during the voting day, simply to cast a ballot). This type of process is completely alien to any left-wing notion of party democracy, but it was worse because Tsipras was the only candidate. It was like: 'I call on my fans to vote for me'. There were 150,000 people who went and voted for Tsipras, and after that, anyone who tried to challenge him in the party faced the argument: '150,000 people voted for him. How many voted for you?' So he became more and more powerful, and he built something that was more like an electoral cartel than a party, including former Pasok politicians and their clientelist networks in some unions or in local government, state bureaucrats, former army officials, lifestyle media personalities and so on. Even some former New Democracy politicians joined or allied with Syriza.

I would say the transformation had already started before 2015 and it was accelerated while in power. By now, you could say it's complete. Words like 'capitalist' or 'working class' are no longer part of Syriza's vocabulary, which now refers to notions like 'the nation' and 'entrepreneurship'. Only the name is the same. It is telling that, now, there is talk about re-founding the party, which is probably implying that they could even change the name to get rid of the references to the radical left. The term 'left' has already receded to the background, replaced by the 'progressive camp'.

This was presented as an electoral strategy where they aimed to get their best electoral results by broadening Syriza to the centre and to the right. It was more than that; it was a strategic shift. And yet, this broadening didn't work out, even electorally. The electoral collapse in the 2023 election was spectacular. We knew they couldn't win, but no one thought that it would be such a defeat. There are many reasons for it. Their opposition to the government was a non-opposition, actually. A moderate in Syriza said that it was the most consensual opposition we've seen since the fall of the military junta. But the main thing is – and that's where 2015 comes in – there is a complete loss of credibility. No one trusts Syriza, no matter what they say they will or they will not do.

So all these factors were important in explaining the collapse. But I'm not sure about Syriza's future and if they can even survive, at least as a major party. That is because Syriza never had the strong roots that Pasok used to have in the working class and in the unions. It didn't have time to build such links. They don't even have the benefit of memories of a good reformist period while in power, like the ones that served Pasok electorally for years. Workers don't have any recollection of the good times of Syriza in power. They won power, they signed the memorandum, there were four more years of austerity, and then they were out of power. There is no positive recollection, even in terms of reformist consciousness, that things were better back then. So it's hard to tell if they can rebound in the future.

Tsipras realised that and resigned from party chair, subsequently choosing to remain silent and retreat from publicity for now, maybe hoping for a future comeback under more favourable conditions. The succession of Tsipras was the culmination of the degeneration. It was decided that, first, they will vote for a new leader; and only after that will they hold a congress to debate their political direction! The voting process was the one established to enable Tsipras in the past: anyone could pay two euros to register and vote. In this non-party, it was also revealed that anyone can run for the leadership.

Stefanos Kasselakis is a 35-year-old entrepreneur who lived in the USA until last June and was completely unknown in Greece until then. He was invited by Tsipras to stand on Syriza's ballot as an ally in the last national elections. That was his only connection to Syriza (and Greek society and politics in general) until last August, when Tsipras resigned, and Kasselakis suddenly declared that he would move to Greece and claim the leadership of the party! Thousands of two-euro 'members' showed up and voted for him in the first round, giving him 45 percent against candidates who had a serious background as leading members of the party. It looks like a shocking hijack by an alien, but the roots lay in the organisational and political degeneration of Syriza, which made this possible.

Kasselakis is simply promising some vague yet extreme 'makeover of the party' and posing as the one who can beat current Prime Minister Mitsotakis. The return to governmental power as an end in itself, electoralist calculations as the main guide for tactics, and the focus on the persona of the leader are all habits that were cultivated by Syriza's leadership, and Kasselakis emerged as an extreme symptom. Nikos Filis, former minister of education and leading member of Syriza, referring to a trend that started under Tsipras and has intensified under Kasselakis, recently lamented on the Greek political TV program Kontra24: 'the cult of the leader, which had a name on it, has now evolved into Messianism, which also has a name on it'.

WHAT ASSESSMENT DO YOU HAVE OF THE ORIENTATION OF THE REVOLUTIONARY LEFT BACK IN 2015, WITH THE BENEFIT OF EIGHT YEARS OF HINDSIGHT?

I don't want to sound arrogant, but I wouldn't change the main choices we made, both in relation to the Syriza experience in general and during 2015. In terms of the Syriza experience, I think the most important thing was the way we in the Internationalist Workers' Left tried to intervene by retaining our independence, organisationally, politically and ideologically.

In terms of the tactics in 2015, we could talk about how fast maybe we should have reacted in terms of the final episodes that led to the split, but I can't find fault – or not a major one – in the way we operated in 2015. I would say there are lessons, but from choices that I stand by.

In addition to being independent in such a formation as Syriza,

I think one of the most important decisions we took as an organisation, as the elections loomed on the road to 2015, was the choice to remain independent from the state and the government. It was an organisational decision that forbade any member to take up any post at any level of government. Of course, we wouldn't be offered some ministry due to our size, but when a party wins power, there are all kinds of positions for anyone willing to take up a position at both low and middle levels of government and the state bureaucracy. Demonstrating independence from the state and the government is an important thing to hold onto. Also, the critique of the government from day one, and the many instances of open differentiation in parliament whenever it was needed during those months, I think those are the important things of our tactics in 2015.

In terms of how fast our reaction was, I think that there is a criticism, or self-criticism, because it involves all the radical left in 2015. We failed to break the climate of 'wait and see' in the working class. It was six months of passivity. I don't know if we had the size to change this. But I recall that everyone, even outside Syriza, seemed content not to try hard enough to change the mood. So you could say that we should have focused more on that. It's a given that we failed, given the outcome. But again, I can't say that if – it's a big 'what if' – we had focused more on the streets, then the working class would have risen. Probably not. But that's one point of focus for reflection.

In terms of the events of Spring–Summer 2015, the opposition in Syriza reacted slowly. Tsipras dictated the terms and the pace of events, and the opposition always reacted to what he did or didn't do. In that sense, it could have moved more boldly and faster and taken up the initiative. Even in the streets during this time, it was so obvious that, at that point, the struggle was inside Syriza. In the absence of a movement, what mattered was the struggle in the party. But there was a lack of initiative on this front in terms of the left-wing opposition as a whole.

In terms of the revolutionary left and DEA and the Red Network, again I'm not sure, meaning that there is a question of whether we should have moved on at the pace that we thought was best, being more aggressive and faster. We did try that as a Red Network, with open criticisms and warnings about where the government was heading, by organising public meetings to discuss the need for a new initiative. But in terms of the split itself, we thought that it would be best to wait for the rest of the opposition to be persuaded to move – to organise the biggest split possible, even if it meant this not happening as or when we would prefer. That was a constant issue we faced over about six months.

There is a saying that the vanguard should be one step ahead of the class, but not yet too far away from the class, so it can march with it and lead it. In the specific context of our relations with the rest of Syriza, how to make this general guide a complete tactic was a permanent, difficult question for us during those six months. How fast should we move? Are Syriza members and workers ready to move? Should we move now? Though I can't tell for sure that, if our argument for a more active approach had prevailed in the whole opposition in Syriza, this would have changed the course of events. Maybe the day after the split could have been even more favourable than it was.

In terms of the left-wing government, which is a separate question, I think that 2012 might have been a bigger opportunity for the revolutionary left if Syriza had won power back then. The struggles were still on; there was a militant mood. The ruling class was not prepared; no one was prepared! No one expected Syriza to do so well in the election of 2012. Even the leadership of Syriza wasn't prepared, which would have also been a good thing for us. It would have been more of an adventure.

In the three years that followed, Syriza had time to prepare – preparing to find compromise and reach out to the ruling class behind closed doors, in meetings and so on. The ruling class was also in preparation. Electoralism prevailed. You had a party of power, in waiting.

At that point, we still defended the goal of a left-wing government in two senses. One was, it was like our banner of what an actual left-wing government would mean. It was the banner under which we fought the actual existing government that Tsipras was planning for. Sometimes it was semantics, it was terms. Tsipras started talking about the government of national salvation and the government of social emergency, and stopped talking about the government of the left, on which we insisted as an alternative project. Of course, it was not just about the terms, we insisted on what an actual – I don't know how to put it – left-wing government should do.

But secondly, and most importantly, by that time, we understood that it's a process that the Greek working class should go through, meaning that it would happen. So we were forced to go through that stage. As optimism is in our DNA, we hoped for the best-case scenario. Not in terms of what Syriza would do, but in terms of a revival of class struggle, raised expectations and demands, a mood in the workers that would roughly say: 'Now that our guys are in power, let's demand everything'. Which was not the case at all, as it turned out. That was our understanding for the left-wing government, after 2012.

In more general terms, after 2015 we argued that it's a slogan that cannot be raised anytime, anyplace. We knew and argued that even before the experience of 2015. Of course, the slogan can remain relevant in certain conditions, or if not the slogan, acknowledging the fact that this is an eventuality that demands from revolutionaries to organise different tactics in such a situation.

In terms of hoping for a best-case scenario, one that could push revolutionaries to engage more with such a prospect rather than simply elaborating a different set of tactics than the usual: after the experience of 2015, we argued that, in order for such a project – the emergence of a left-wing government – to have a positive side effect in the escalation of class struggle, there should be a much higher level of self-confidence and self-organisation in the class.

That's something that we underestimated when hoping for the best in 2015: that the working class, its self-confidence and its organisations – organisations that are autonomous from the state and with a confidence to act despite the state – were not strong enough. That's one thing that I think matters.

The other is the relation of forces on the left itself: a stronger revolutionary left or even a stronger radical opposition that was more politically clear and with stronger links with the working class can be an important precondition. That was another problem that I implied before – that we didn't have the size to mobilise the class as a counterweight to what Tsipras' forces were doing.

Those were the main two preconditions in terms of being able to make the best of a situation of the government of the left.

I've spoken about our tactics, but there was also a section of the revolutionary left that chose to abstain from joining Syriza and the fight inside it. They were active outside it. However, at least in terms of success for their own forces, it didn't work. Their estimation – that when the prophecy that Syriza will betray comes true, then the working class will realise they were right all along and follow them – didn't materialise.

The defeat is one reason. Defeats can offer valuable lessons for the more politicised activists. It's our task to communicate these lessons to a broader audience. But, at the time they happen, such political and social defeats are not the best environment for a further radicalisation in broader parts of the working class.

Of course, I want to distinguish Antarsya from the Communist Party. The comrades in Antarsya had a more active approach to events in 2015. For example, they were present in the rallies of February. These rallies had a mixed, contradictory mood: they were in support of the government against the blackmailers in the EU. So it was support for the government, but also pushing the government not to retreat, not to capitulate. Antarsya was present in these demonstrations. And, of course, in the referendum itself, we worked with comrades in Antarsya very closely in this fight. They knew, and we knew, that no one could trust Tsipras. But we realised the importance of this struggle.

It was not the same as what the Communist Party did, which is a counter example of complete passivity in the face of major events. We usually identify sectarianism with ultra leftism, but you can be sectarian because you are deeply conservative. That's the case with the Greek Communist Party back then.

Back to the revolutionary left: there's a debate even to this day with comrades of Antarsya that can never be resolved. There is the argument that, if Antarsya had joined the opposition inside Syriza early on, the fight inside Syriza could have been stronger. And the comrades of Antarsya insist that, if we had left Syriza early on and joined Antarsya, the revolutionary left would be stronger as an independent force.

For me, there is a more intriguing 'what if' which goes back to 2010, at the beginning of this turbulent period – when Antarsya rejected an approach by the left wing of Syriza, which was on the verge of splitting the party back then. It didn't materialise, and we will never know how events would have evolved with such a different alignment in the Greek left.

On the never-ending debate around tactics after 2012, I agree with the first position, that Antarsya could have made more of an impact by allying with the left-wing opposition in Syriza. I think that, at some point, it looked like class struggle itself was – in a very peculiar way – being waged inside Syriza. In the absence of actual class struggle, what mattered in 2015 was what was happening inside the party. The mainstream press realised it, the creditors realised it, all the debate was focused on what Tsipras was doing, what would he do, and how we – the opposition – would react in the party.

So I think it was a mistake to abstain from that battle. In order to be more relevant to people that followed Syriza – not only members, but supporters – Antarsya failed to build such links by choosing to abstain from that front. All kinds of tactics were tried inside Syriza, outside Syriza and even outside Antarsya. If we look at our situation today, no one won in terms of organisational growth. Maybe that's a different topic.

I will talk about the part of the revolutionary left that was inside Syriza and adopted a different tactic than ours: the Communist Organisation of Greece. They were in Syriza. They were the biggest group of the Greek revolutionary left. They were way bigger than us. They chose a very different tactic by being part of the leading group and remaining close to Tsipras as a more loyal opposition, dissolving their group in 2013, when we refused to do so. They still technically exist on paper but, in reality, they are non-existent. That is, a big group of the revolutionary left collapsed because of the tactics they pursued inside Syriza. Many of them remained in Syriza. Others left, completely demoralised, and went home. The few that remain in the group have embarked on a 'post-left' journey.

In contrast, when we exited Syriza, and for some time after that, we were actually in the best shape that I have seen the group, DEA, in since I joined in 2006. So, in terms of growing as a group and building links with a broader audience (the Red Network), I think our tactics in Syriza worked.

The problem is what happened after that. All the revolutionary left groups went into crisis in the following years. It is the aftermath of the defeat and the failure of Popular Unity, which was founded in 2015 after the split from Syriza. This is a broader subject, but I think that, for the far left, it was the failure of Popular Unity that provoked crisis and led to smaller sized organisations for all of us. That was our defeat.

The split itself, both as a split in Syriza and in terms of the revolutionary left and its apex in Syriza, I think was a success. The party broke in half at all levels. It was a huge thing at that time. The failure came afterwards – the failure to build an alternative. We lacked our main fuel, the class struggle. There were political mistakes in Popular Unity – many political mistakes – that we failed to fight against or win.

But the main problem was something that Antonis Davanellos, a leading member of DAE, used to say in the years leading up to 2015, when explaining the rise of Syriza to comrades abroad: the class struggle in Greece had been very generous to the left. It was not some tricks or some special charisma of Syriza. Class struggle was very generous to the Greek left from 2006 up to 2015. Then it stopped being generous. We were spoiled in always having strong movements and radicalisation. In the absence of that, building a new alternative failed, and that's when all the revolutionary left went into crisis.

I think all groups have been through a split during the past few years. At the start, the debates were about what went wrong, why did we lose etc. You know, defeats always cause more discontent. However, as I've already said, the movement is on the rebound, especially among younger people not burdened by that defeat, but also veterans who try to move again. There are reasons for a certain optimism, despite a dire situation. We still have many groups of revolutionaries left in Greece. We are not in the state we used to be, but we have shared an important experience and, hopefully, we are trying to find some common ground in our evaluation of that period.

Those both inside Syriza and outside Syriza, we are the forces that still can serve as the starting point for something new and more radical, by finding a common understanding of what happened and our self-criticisms. There has been self-criticism in parts of Antarsya, for example. Everyone realises that no one can be arrogant about their past political line 100 percent.

So this process of maturing and finding common ground today, I hope can be the basis for the Greek far left to work together to rebuild our forces. No one can do it on their own; there are many groups in Greece. So working together is a big gateway if you want to do something. So I think that was a process of maturing, let's say, for all of us.

August 2023

FURTHER READING

Ovenden, Kevin, *Syriza: Inside the Labyrinth,* Pluto Press, 2015.

Roos, Jerome, *Why not Default? the Political Economy of Sovereign Debt,* Princeton University Press, 2019.

Sheehan, Helena, *The Syriza Wave: Surging and Crashing with the Greek Left,* Monthly Review Press, 2017.

Varoufakis, Yanis, *Adults in the Room: My Battle with Europe's Deep Establishment*, Vintage, 2017

GLOSSARY

ANEL - Anexartitoi Ellines, National Patriotic Alliance. 2012 nationalist split from New Democracy

Antarsya - Antikapitalistiki Aristeri Synergasia gia tin Anatropi, Front of the Greek Anticapitalist Left. Left-wing coalition founded 2009

Davanellos, Antonis - Leading member of DEA

DEA - Diethnistiki Ergatiki Aristera, Internationalist Workers' Left. Founded in 2001 after a split from the Socialist Workers' Party (SEK) - the Greek section of the International Socialist Tendency

EAM - Ethnikó Apeleftherotikó Métopo, National Liberation Front, main movement of Greek resistance to the Nazis

ECB - European Central Bank

ELA - Emergency Liquidity Assistance; emergency financial assistance provided by the European Central Bank

Eurogroup - Term for informal meetings of the finance ministers of the eurozone

George Papandreou - Greek Prime Minister 2009–2011, member of Pasok

Golden Dawn - Neo-Nazi political party

IMF - International Monetary Fund

Internationalist Workers' Left - Leading force in the Left Platform inside Syriza. See DEA

KKE - Kommounistikó Kómma Elládas, Communist Party of Greece

KOE - Kommounistikí Orgánosi Elládas, Communist Organisation of Greece. Founded in 2003, with roots in the KKE

Kasselakis, Stefanos - Greek–American entrepreneur elected leader of Syriza in 2023

LAE - Laïkí Enótita - Anipótakti Aristera. See Popular Unity

Lafazanis, Panagiotis - Syriza minister for production and reorganisation, leading member of the Left Current and a founder of Popular Unity

Left Platform - Left grouping inside Syriza comprising both DEA and Left Current

Memorandum - Loan repayment agreement

Military junta - Known as the Regime of the Colonels. Right-wing military dictatorship that ruled Greece from 1967 to 1974

Mitsotakis, Kyriakos - New Democracy Prime Minister 2019 to present

NEI - Greek for Yes. Pronounced 'nay'. Protagonists arguing for a Yes vote on the memorandum of agreement

New Democracy - Conservative Party, in government between 2012 and 2015

OXI - Greek for No. Pronounced 'ochee' with ch as in loch. Became a main slogan during 2015, and signified a call for a No vote on the memorandum of agreement negotiated between Europe's financial institutions and the Greek Government

Panitch, Leo - Academic political scientist and co-editor of *Socialist Register*

Papandreou, Andreas - Founder and leader of Pasok. First Pasok prime minister

Pasok - Panellínio Sosialistikó Kínima, Panhellenic Socialist Movement

Popular Unity - Political party formed after the Left Platform and 25 MPs split from Syriza. Known by its Greek initials LAE

Red Network - One of two left-wing factions comprising the Left Platform within Syriza

Samaras, Antonis - Greek Prime Minister 2012–2015, member of New Democracy

Synaspismós - Eurocommunist split from the KKE

Syntagma Square - Central square in Athens, starting point of demonstrations and political protests

Syriza - Synaspismós Rizospastikís Aristerás – Proodeftikí Simachía, Coalition of the Radical Left. Left-wing party formed 2004

To Potami - The River. Neoliberal political party formed 2014

Troika - Group of three creditors: the International Monetary Fund, European Commission and ECB

Tsipras, Alexis - Greek Prime Minister 2015–2019, member of Syriza

Varoufakis, Yannis - Economist, joined Syriza as finance minister

VAT - Value Added Tax

Žižek, Slavoj - Slovenian philosopher

BIOGRAPHIES

Colleen Bolger is a member of Socialist Alternative in Australia. She has stood as a candidate for the Victorian Socialists in several elections. She is also a lawyer who acts for people with asbestos-related and occupational diseases and is a delegate with the Australian Services Union.

Panos Petrou is a member of the Central Committee of the Internationalist Workers' Left (DEA by its Greek acronym). He edits the organisation's newspaper, *Workers' Left*, and its periodical journal, *Kokkino* ('Red').

Tia Kasambalis is a Walkley-nominated artist and illustrator working out of the Victorian Trades Hall Art Studio, Naarm (Melbourne) and a member of the Workers Art Collective – a group of left-wing artists creating content for the workers' movement. He has published work in *The Saturday Paper*, *Overland Journal*, *The Lifted Brow* and for SBS and the Asylum Seeker Resource Centre. You can find his work on Instagram at @tia_kass.

ABOUT INTERVENTIONS

Interventions is an independent, not-for-profit, incorporated publisher. We publish left-wing, radical and socialist books by Australian authors. We welcome books which for political or financial reasons are unlikely to be accepted by commercial publishers. Our books cover a wide range of topics including labour history, left-wing politics, radical cultural themes, socialism and Marxism, memoirs, and works about resistance to racism, sexism and all other forms of oppression.

At Interventions we believe radical ideas matter. We want our books to be part of the development of a critical and engaged Australian left.

By highlighting alternative voices, especially those that have been pushed to the margins, we hope to contribute to a greater insight and awareness of the injustices that exist in society, and the many efforts at the grassroots to right these wrongs.

We welcome publishing proposals. If you are interested in submitting a proposal please check out the information for authors on our website https://interventions.org.au/forauthors. If you think your proposal fits our guidelines please follow the submission process outlined there. Please note we are not currently publishing poetry or fiction.

Interventions has no independent source of income and is committed to keeping prices accessible. As bookshops and warehouses close around the world, our future hangs in the balance. By supporting us you will help us keep radical ideas alive and accessible to all. If you would like to support radical publishing in Australia please consider supporting our Patreon. Visit patreon.com/interventions to donate a small amount each month and get some great rewards.

Website: https://interventions.org.au/

Contact us: info@interventions.org.au or use the contact form on the website.

ABOUT THIS BOOK

This book was edited by Ben Hillier and the Interventions production project manager was Janey Stone. Tess Lee Ack assisted with proof reading.

This book was copy edited by Eris Harrison of Effective Editing.

This book was designed and laid out by Viktoria Ivanova. Viktoria is a communication designer in Melbourne. She is a book publishing fiend, runs Spark Publishing Inc (for art-centric left books) and also designs for Victorian Socialists.

All images in this book are by photographer Tia Kasambalis who is a Walkley nominated artist and illustrator working out of the Victorian Trades Hall Art Studio, and a member of the Workers Art Collective. You can find his work on Instagram at @tia_kass.

The Art of Rebellion: Dispatches from Hong Kong 2015

By Ben Hillier

....

'A series of extraordinary dispatches offering an intimate portrait of a twenty-first century insurgency, a movement that's violent and tender, confused and yet incredibly inspiring. In prose so urgent that you can smell tear gas on each page, Hillier eschews the voyeurism of the revolutionary tourist to investigate instead what the art of rebellion might mean – both for Hong Kong and for radicals all over the world.'

-Jeff Sparrow, writer and broadcaster

'In a wonderful introduction to the art of rebellion, Ivanova has curated more than one hundred artworks produced during the recent uprising. the pieces – not merely about the struggle, but indivisible from it – are in constant dialogue with Hillier's clear-eyed, crystalising reportage, and allow the streets to speak for themselves. the diverse collection, not necessarily intended for publication or posterity, gives form and soul to the sometimes abstract and nebulous world of politics.'

-Sam Wallman, comics-journalist, cartoonist and labour activist

MORE FROM INTERVENTIONS

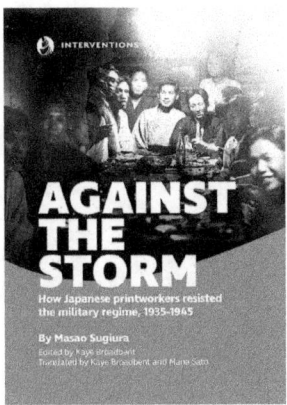

Losing Santhia: Life and loss in the struggle for Tamil Eelam

By Ben Hillier

'A remarkable essay... All those interested in contemporary struggles for self-determination should read this.'
-Gill H Boehringer, former head of Macquarie University law school

....

On a small stretch of sand in north-eastern Sri Lanka 2009, the armed forces slaughtered tens of thousands of Tamils. The Tamil Tigers, who had waged a three-decade-long war of national liberation, were militarily defeated. But some of their ranks survived. Santhia was one. After the war, she and her infant son tried to reach Australia but were stranded in Indonesia. Santhia died in a Jakarta hospital in October 2017 aged just forty-two.

Sponsored by the Tamil Refugee Council, Ben Hillier travelled to Indonesia and Sri Lanka after Santhia's death to piece together her life. In this essay, she appears as an individual expression of a nation's fight for liberation. The essay is paired with a seminal document, Liberation Tigers and Tamil Eelam freedom struggle, written in 1983 by Anton Balasingham on behalf of the Tigers' political committee.

Against the Storm: How Japanese printworkers resisted the military regime 1935-1945

By Masao Sugiura
Edited by Kaye Broadbent
Translated by Kaye Broadbent and Mana Sato

'In doing what is normal for any trade union activist today -- recruiting, arguing and organising -- my comrades and I were made to suffer persecution, imprisonment and death.'

....

This inspiring memoir tells how young Japanese print and publishing workers maintained links and sustained organisation between workers during the height of Japanese military aggression before and during World War II. It destroys the myth that ordinary Japanese people all supported the war, and provides a thrilling account of worker organising in conditions of repression that has lessons for the up-and-coming unionists of today.

www.ingramcontent.com/pod-product-compliance
Lightning Source LLC
Chambersburg PA
CBHW071958290426
44109CB00018B/2063